Treasure Baskets and

Treasure Baskets and Beyond

Realizing the Potential of Sensory-rich Play

Sue Gascoyne

 Open University Press

Open University Press
McGraw-Hill Education
McGraw-Hill House
Shoppenhangers Road
Maidenhead
Berkshire
England
SL6 2QL

email: enquiries@openup.co.uk
world wide web: www.openup.co.uk

and Two Penn Plaza, New York, NY 10121–2289, USA

First published 2012

A catalogue record of this book is available from the British Library

ISBN-13: 978-0-33-524644-1 (pb)
ISBN-10: 0-33-524644-3 (pb)
eISBN: 978-0-33-524645-8

Library of Congress Cataloging-in-Publication Data
CIP data applied for

Typesetting and e-book compilations by
RefineCatch Limited, Bungay, Suffolk
Printed and bound by CPI Group (UK) Ltd, Croydon, CR0 4YY

The **McGraw·Hill** Companies

In loving memory of my Dad

Contents

List of figures and tables   x
Preface   xi
Acknowledgements   xii
Foreword   xiii

 1 **Introducing sensory-rich play**   1
 2 **Our amazing senses**   17
 3 **The world of objects**   37
 4 **Introducing Treasure Baskets and heuristic play**   52
 5 **Introducing the Sensory Play Continuum**   77
 6 **The Sensory Play Continuum in action**   89
 7 **Bringing the curriculum alive**   108
 8 **Sensory processing and special educational needs**   123
 9 **Adults – getting the balance right**   139
10 **Conclusion: Treasure Baskets – a twenty-first
     century resource?**   160
    Appendix 1: Treasure Basket observation template   164

    References   166
    Index   173

List of figures and tables

Figures

Figure 1.1	Nature for the child is sheer sensory experience	9
Figure 2.1	Exploring treasures is an all-encompassing experience	24
Figure 3.1	A carefully crafted Treasure Basket	39
Figure 4.1	Selecting Treasure Basket objects with sensory appeal	56
Figure 4.2	Treasure Basket play involves full-bodied exploration	65
Figure 5.1	Combining resources ensures hands-on learning through play	80
Figure 6.1	Sensory-rich resources like these offer age-appropriate play and learning opportunities	105
Figure 7.1	Problem solving in action	116
Figure 9.1	The interplay between environment, adult and child	140
Figure 9.2	Adults' role in the Sensory Play Continuum	157

Tables

Table 1.1	The Sensory Play Continuum	16
Table 2.1	The senses	19
Table 2.2	Taxonomy of exploratory hand procedures	25
Table 2.3	Stages of sensory perception	35
Table 4.1	Maximizing the sensory appeal of Treasure Baskets	57
Table 5.1	The affordance of objects	82
Table 5.2	Resources for combining with Treasure Basket objects	83
Table 5.3	Treasure Basket activities	87
Table 8.1	Improving access to a Treasure Basket using the Sensory Play Continuum	135
Appendix 1	Treasure Basket observation template	164

Preface

My first foray into the intoxicating world of sensory play began with a Treasure Basket, and so it's apt for this to be the starting point for this book. Even before my first child was born my enlightened mother-in-law had introduced me to Treasure Baskets, and although I didn't fully understand and appreciate their huge benefit and potential then, I was immediately sold on the idea. Since those early days of watching my baby daughter exploring and playing with a Treasure Basket I too have embarked on a journey of discovery and reflection. For the first two years of her life I continued to add to her Treasure Basket and offer it for play. As she played for protracted periods of time, deeply engrossed, I extolled the virtues of Treasure Baskets to my friends, but they rarely shared my enthusiasm for a basket of seemingly disparate objects, opting for plastic toys instead. The full potential of this resource only really dawned on me when her baby brother began exploring his own Treasure Basket. Without any prompting she delved beneath her bed to bring out her Treasure Basket and sat next to him playing with her treasures. As I watched my three-and-a-half-year-old and six-month-old playing side by side with similar objects, but in very different ways, I glimpsed the true potential of a Treasure Basket.

In my quest to understand better the appeal and benefits of this type of play I have instigated several research projects which have helped shape my thinking. The first of these, *The Sensory Play Research Project* (Papatheodorou 2010), provided an insight into how adults' views of play have changed, as well as a number of play observations in a range of Early Years settings using the Sensory Play Continuum. Observations of Treasure Basket play have helped consolidate my belief that this type of open-ended collection of sensory-rich objects offers something special for children across the ages. Preliminary findings from a pilot research project to map brain activity in 3- to 4-year-olds during Treasure Basket play (Khan 2011) helps cast a lens on the wonders of the brain. I have also carried out over 20 observations of Treasure Basket play sessions in an Activity Centre to test emerging thinking further. The culmination of these can be found in the pages of this book and will, I hope, provide even the most ardent Treasure Basket enthusiast with further 'food for thought' as well as converting some critics! I for one am grateful for the discoveries that I have made and the lessons learnt from countless observations of Treasure Basket play.

Acknowledgements

My thanks go to Marianne Gascoyne for introducing me to Treasure Baskets and supporting me in my endeavours. The staff and children at Jungle Adventure, Lilliput Village Nursery, Nannas Day Nursery, Old Heath Community Pre-school and Primary School, Orchard Barns Private Kindergarten, Redcliffe Children's Centre, Woodland Children's Centre and Mary Byrne have made some fascinating observations which have contributed both to the development of the book and conveying its message. I am also grateful to Janet Moyles, Theodora Papatheodorou and Katrin Stroh for generously sharing their time and views, to Dan, my Mum and family for their unfaltering support and belief, and to Freya and Zachary for their boundless inspiration.

Foreword

Janet Moyles

For several years, early childhood educators have used the concept of 'Treasure Baskets' to enrich the multi-sensory experiences of babies and very young children. From Elinor Goldschmied's and her colleagues' original inspiration[1] over thirty years ago, many practitioners have developed Treasure Baskets in different ways and there is now a wealth of practical ideas available for stimulating babies' and young children's sensory and heuristic play and learning. 'Heuristic play is founded in children's natural curiosity and their drive to manipulate through all their senses'[2] and is an important part of children developing both manipulative capabilities and confidence in handling a range of materials, textures, smells, tastes, sounds and sights. These sensory experiences provide the foundation for all learning.

It is well researched that any 'toys' provided for children should be flexible so that children can use them in a variety of imaginative and creative ways, e.g. construction toys, clay, sand, water and, of course, Treasure Basket contents. If we want future citizens who can think creatively and flexibly, they must practise varied skills from an early age. Flexible materials start this process. It is known that children in all societies will use anything to hand as a 'toy' – babies love saucepans and wooden spoons so why would we buy a plastic drum and stick which limit a baby's textural experience and understanding? What is important to play is any kind of flexible material which children can use in their own way without restriction – a tablecloth or old curtain can become a cape; a large cardboard box can become a den; pieces of wood or logs can be used to build climbing frames. In the case of babies and young children, the Treasure Basket can provide an immediate and entertaining experience, supporting concentration and neural development to mention but two aspects.

Exploration is about first-hand experiences, trial-and-error learning and sensory encounters. Children engaged through their play in exploring the world, learn to develop a perception of themselves as competent, self-assured learners who know that it's all right to ask questions, make mistakes and discover things for themselves. Whilst gathering information about objects through exploration, children acquire skills including problem-solving and understanding of the characteristics of each object.

With pressure on children from an ever earlier age, a book such as this by Sue Gascoyne, puts into perspective the need for babies, toddlers and all young children to have a plethora of extensive sensory play experiences before any expectation is put upon them to 'conform' to formal educational situations. The author highlights the uniqueness of each individual child and explores in some depth just how much and how many broad-based experiences of objects and materials children must have before their brains and bodies are sufficiently developed to progress to higher levels of functioning. Whilst not downplaying the need for object play, the author stresses the wider significance of sensory play to children's development and to meeting the needs of individual children.

Whereas most books written about Treasure Baskets are very practical – and there are certainly many useful suggestions for practice made in this book –Sue Gascoyne's book redresses the need for one which offers additionally an abundance of theoretical and research evidence including her own. From examining the range and depth of babies' and children's senses and their biological need for stimulating experiences, the author goes on to explore the rationale underpinning the use of Treasure Baskets for children well into primary school age, a unique and enthralling aspect of the book. This very different slant strongly supports the influence of Treasure Baskets on children's sensory-rich experiences right across the early years and well into the primary phase of education and links closely with all children's opportunities for understanding and knowledge acquisition through personal meaning-making.

Whilst many of the concepts and scientific knowledge presented, such as that from neuroscience, may seemingly appear fairly abstract, Sue Gascoyne has skilfully woven them into an accessible 'story' in the ten chapters presented in this book. Like her predecessor, Elinor Goldschmied, Sue clearly believes that children should have access to any type of material beyond plastic! This may mean that, at times, practitioners may fear for children's safety, for example, when a six-month old puts a metal object such as a chain into her mouth or holds a heavy glass ball. The world around us is an exciting place and babies, like older children, need to find out about objects and the relationship they have to themselves and others. We all have to acknowledge that, in the risk averse society in which we live, without the opportunity to be adventurous in an age-appropriate way, children cannot learn to keep themselves safe and feel capable and competent. Learning self-efficacy begins early and needs constant achievement to be sustained so that all children reach their learning potential. Sue emphasises that every child can play with a Treasure Basket and so gain valuable knowledge and information from its everyday contents through hands-on, real life, fun experiences under the guidance of caring but flexible adults.

Many practitioners believe that babies and young children have very short concentration spans: a particular aspect of Treasure Basket play as explained by the author is the concentration so apparent in even the youngest child. Valuable insights into why this is so are given in the book and practitioners are supported in documenting this and other developmental aspects through Sue Gascoyne's *Sensory Play Continuum*. Her observations of Treasure Basket play across birth-to-aged eight years plus are fascinating and certainly offer a wealth of implicit and explicit guidance for practitioners wanting to extend their understanding and practice of Treasure Basket play. Chapter 2, exploring our amazing senses, will feed practitioners with much needed support for explaining the benefits of sensory play to others including parents and carers.

Seemingly very simple, different forms of Treasure Basket can offer different experiences, as Sue carefully explains through both words and delightful photographs. Practitioners will appreciate the useful activities offered in each chapter to support their understanding of different elements of Treasure Basket play, aspects of which can be surprisingly challenging. Readers should not be fooled into thinking that Treasure Baskets are simply a matter of putting a few objects in a natural wicker basket! Throughout the book, Sue Gascoyne highlights the important role of practitioners in making provision (especially culturally relevant basket contents) but also in observing and guiding (from a distance) Treasure Basket play and accepting that the play may well be very flexible and offer the unexpected in terms of children's responses.

The links the author makes between sensory play, schemas and early years curricula demonstrate clearly the importance of practitioners not getting too caught up in 'delivery' mode without considering the individual needs of the children and their previous sensory experiences. The importance of recognising the way different children learn is also rightly emphasised by Sue Gascoyne as she sensitively but firmly deals with the issue of child/child and child/adult relationships and the vital role adults have in valuing children's need for time to explore through personal, hands-on experience. My own research has shown that most adults give insufficient time to listening to children's responses to play situations and to observing how they play and their inherent learning.[3] If all adults could be encouraged to do this, they would understand the value of play to children's development.

All forms of play nowadays are frequently goal-focused which actually means that it is not real play at all. Unless children set their own goals, goal-focused play is usually under the ownership of others, e.g. the 'educators', whereas real play is owned by the player him/herself, in this case, the child. There is so little time to be 'a child' in modern society and to act in playful and childlike ways that it seems to me that society should be making every endeavour to offer children a free, happy childhood, rather than a controlled, goal-oriented one. This feeling resonates throughout Sue's impressive and accessible book. It is not only desirable but vital for children to control their own Treasure Basket play thus learning about themselves, their capabilities, limitations and strengths as well as about properties and materials.

This accomplished book represents an impressive and important extension of previous writing in the field and is sure to expand practitioners' understanding of the fascinating medium that is the Treasure Basket.

Notes

1 Jackson, S., Forbes, R. and Goldschmied, E. (1994) *People Under Three:Young Children in Day Care*. London: Routledge.
2 Moyles, J. (2012) *The A to Z of Play in Early Childhood*. Maidenhead: Open University Press/McGraw Hill.
3 Moyles, J. and Worthington, M. (2011) *The Early Years Foundation Stage through the daily experiences of children*. TACTYC Occasional paper No: 1. Available online at: www.tactyc.org.uk/occasionalpapers.asp (accessed 2nd April, 2012).

1 Introducing sensory-rich play

Everything we know about the world and ourselves has come through our senses

(Bogdashina, *Sensory Perceptual Issues in Autism and Asperger Syndrome*)

Overview

This chapter sets Treasure Baskets within a wider theoretical and sensory context, making links with the worlds of neuroscience and outdoor play. It introduces the six dimensions of 'beyond' which form the focus of the book, suggesting far greater significance to Treasure Basket play than initially meets the eye.

Treasure Baskets and beyond

If ever there was a resource that combines simplicity and sophistication, both enthralling children and bemusing adults, it is the Treasure Basket. Essentially a basket of natural and household objects, the Treasure Basket of Elinor Goldschmied's creation has the senses at its very core. In essence 'babies use their five senses along with their co-ordination of eye and hand in playing with objects, which in their various ways offer them a rich stimulus' (Goldschmied 1989, cited in Forbes 2004: 62). Its inception was influenced by Goldschmied's own childhood experiences, growing up as she did in the countryside, with the environment's natural treasures, her playthings of choice. Satisfied by nature's 'instruments for exploration and imagination' (Hughes 2006: 7), Goldschmied sought to distil this very essence into a resource which would be accessible to the urban child too, and so the Treasure Basket was 'born'. Some seventy years later, its links to sensory play have been largely forgotten, with Treasure Baskets more closely associated with heuristic play than their sensory roots. This brings me to the book's title – *Treasure Baskets and Beyond* – to explain from the outset what this means and to introduce the six dimensions of 'beyond' which form the focus of this book.

1 The importance of sensory play

Despite its sensory origins the Treasure Basket has largely become synonymous in the early years sector with heuristic play (discovery play with lots of objects, to which we will return shortly). Limiting the application of Treasure Baskets in this way loses some of their wider significance for children's development. Understanding the importance of the senses in the early years is critical to meeting children's needs, as we shall discover in Chapter 2. So too is a full appreciation of the value and appeal of sensory-rich play, and recognition that children's play is changing. Unstructured play (particularly outdoors) is in danger of being squeezed out in favour of organized clubs and screen-based alternatives (Gill 2011; Play England 2011). Recognizing the importance of the senses as a gateway to all learning is fundamental to tailoring appropriate provision, essential for fulfilling children's potential. It is also crucial to meeting the needs of children with sensory processing difficulties who, as we shall discover in Chapter 8, experience the world in a fundamentally different way.

2 Understanding babies' brains

Until recently, babies were predominantly viewed as helpless entities to be nurtured and protected from the environment. As we shall discover in Chapter 2, advances in neuroscience are beginning to challenge such mainstream perceptions, portraying babies as remarkably sophisticated sensory beings.

3 The benefits and appeal of objects

Few young children can resist the appeal of a Treasure Basket. Superficially the level of engagement and play potential may seem disproportionate to the sum of its parts. A basket of natural and household objects could not be further from the all-singing, all-dancing toys that we have come to expect. Chapter 3 delves beneath the surface of this resource to explore the mysterious appeal of Treasure Baskets. Drawing on the world of object play and its relationship to brain development, the allure and benefits of this type of play are explored and numerous assumptions questioned. Although further research is needed, the apparent simplicity of a Treasure Basket may conceal its importance as a sophisticated 'rule acquisition' tool.

4 The benefits of Treasure Basket play to older children

The concept of a Treasure Basket, developed by Elinor Goldschmied, was for babies aged 7–12 months after which children, once mobile, progressed to heuristic play, i.e. play with lots of similar objects. With children's developmental milestones occurring at different times and every child unique, imposing an age restriction instinctively seems at odds with good practice. In a clear departure from Goldschmied's thinking, this book sets out the case for offering Treasure Baskets to older children. Based on a wealth of observations of Treasure Basket play in Chapters 4, 5 and 6, readers will be invited to make up their own minds about whether this resource should continue to remain the preserve of babies. In Chapter 7 we will explore how sensory-rich resources like Treasure Baskets can help bring the early years curriculum to life, making learning relevant, real and fun.

5 Balancing child-led and adult-led play

A key characteristic of play with a Treasure Basket, as described by Elinor Goldschmied, was that it should be child led. Indeed for the youngest of children this resource offers perhaps the one and only opportunity for them actually to choose what to play with and how. This child-led dimension is a vital characteristic of free play with a Treasure Basket, but it is also an aspect of play that many adults grapple with. Time and time again observations of Treasure Basket play have been characterized by well-meaning adults intervening through comments, suggestions, questions, and imposing their own play ideas. Indeed, if unchecked an emphasis upon active parenting and the adult as a key driver of play threatens the very thing that makes free play with a Treasure Basket so special. In Chapter 9 we explore further the thorny issue of if, when and how to become involved in children's play without destroying its essence. The Sensory Play Continuum (Gascoyne 2009) is explored in Chapters 5 and 6, and offers a tool for safeguarding the special qualities of Treasure Basket play by helping adults achieve this balance.

6 Exploring our sensory preferences

It's all too easy to forget our own sensory preferences and needs, dismissing these as childish or irrelevant. In fact, as numerous practitioner training sessions frequently testify, when as adults we give ourselves time and permission to nurture our own sensory needs we are quickly propelled into childhood memories, as crystal clear as the day the memories were created. Sensory-rich experiences forge memories. It is vital for us to remember this and be aware of our own sensory preferences, assumptions and practice so we can ensure that these are not at odds with the needs of children in our care, particularly those with special educational needs (SEN), as we will discover in Chapter 8. Practitioner reflection is a key aspect of good practice and sensory reflection is no different. In Chapter 9 this will be explored further as part of a toolkit for appraising sensory provision.

Throughout the book we will return to these six 'dimensions of beyond' as drivers not just for enhancing play with a Treasure Basket, but improving play provision generally. I will now briefly introduce the links between Treasure Baskets and sensory play before focusing on the theoretical context.

Introducing Treasure Baskets and sensory play

For something so fundamental to children's growth and development, definitions of sensory play (like play itself) are remarkably elusive! Sensory play is essentially play that engages one or more of the senses. As such, most play clearly has the potential to be sensory. However, sensory play differs from other types of play in that the sensory focus adds a significant and integral extra dimension to the play. Usher (2010: 2) defines sensory play as 'play that provides opportunities for children and young people to use all their senses or opportunities to focus play to encourage the use of one particular sense'. Sensory play is commonly accessed in the outdoor environment, and some forms, like sand and water play, can be intrinsically messy, which for most children only adds to their appeal! Many sensory-rich play opportunities surround us in our everyday lives, from a muddy puddle to a tree root, and most of these are freely or cheaply available.

As Treasure Basket objects are not toys, like the outdoor environment they offer limitless potential for open-ended play. Gibson introduced the idea of 'affordance' of objects or environments in terms of what they can offer. This means 'that what is perceived when looking at objects is not their dimensions or properties but their affordances: what they can provide or offer' (McInnes *et al.* 2011: 123). To an adult, Treasure Basket objects may be seen literally as a collection of household and natural objects but to a child (or playful adult) they can offer a high degree of affordance, much like a tree does in the outdoors environment. Each Treasure Basket object has the potential to be used in a multitude of ways so that with an imaginative mind a metal chain is transformed into a snake, spaghetti, two characters or even an oven! But this resource doesn't just offer individual affordances; the juxtaposition of objects within the basket (many of which you would not expect to find together) also affords countless play and explorative permutations.

Theoretical context

Treasure Baskets, heuristic play and loose parts play

Working in orphanages in 1940s rural Italy, Elinor Goldschmied observed babies' fascination for playing with the simplest of household objects, like those found in a kitchen. From her observations of play, the idea of a Treasure Basket – a basket of natural and household objects, picked for their sensory appeal – was conceived for babies aged 7–12 months. Research and observations of older children playing have since highlighted the value of Treasure Baskets for children aged 6 months to 6 years and even older, as well as children with special educational needs. We will return to this at the end of this chapter when we introduce the Sensory Play Continuum (Gascoyne 2009). The importance of Learning Tools (see Chapter 3) has also emerged as a way of understanding young children's play (Waldon cited in Stroh *et al.* 2008).

In the 1980s the term 'heuristic play', meaning discovery play, was coined by Goldschmied (in conjunction with Anita Hughes and Glen Carmichael). This concept was used to describe the type of exploratory play behaviour seen when 1- to 2-year-olds engage with lots of bags of different objects, such as bags of jam jar lids, curtain hoops and so on (Goldschmied and Jackson 1994). Heuristic play is characterized by children engaging in deeply absorbing repetitive behaviours and trial and error investigations and was felt to be particularly suited to 1- to 2-year-olds with their newly discovered mobility and independence. Unlike Treasure Baskets, heuristic play objects are not picked with sensory interest in mind, but for their availability in quantities that make endless play permutations possible. Less widespread in the early years is loose parts play, the term coined by architect Simon Nicholson in the 1970s for open-ended materials like sand, cardboard boxes, crates, pallets, bakers' trays, tyres, gravel, logs, containers and guttering that can be used in limitless ways. The potential for creativity and open-ended play has close parallels to Treasure Baskets and heuristic play, albeit on a much larger scale, as a beach can be a loose parts environment! Their widespread appeal is also apparent with children aged 1–11 years (and older) enjoying play with resources like these. This also has much in common with Broadhead's 'Whatever you want it to be place' (2004: 73).

Sensory play

Turning to the senses, the theoretical context is less clear, with several theorists recognizing the importance of sensory experiences and environments. A key contributor to the development and understanding of sensory play was Jean Piaget (1896–1980). He believed that children's interactions with their environment create learning, and described the first stage in a child's development as the sensorimotor stage. Occurring in the first two years of life, it is characterized by most learning occurring through the senses and manipulation of objects, the focus of the next two chapters. Piaget introduced the term 'disequilibrium' when a child encounters something unexpected and needs to assimilate and accommodate this new information and learning, something which resonates with recent neuroscience findings. Piaget also believed that babies need to manipulate and explore interesting objects, which has obvious parallels with the types of objects and explorative play associated with a Treasure Basket. In the sensorimotor stage 'children build up a mental picture . . . based on their sensory contact with their environment. They do this when they hold, feel, suck, listen to, look at, shake and throw things' (Beaver *et al.* 1997: 52). Piaget believed that 'words such as "bigger", "smaller", "longer", "further", are not understood until the logical properties themselves are understood' (Geraghty 1990: 96). This would certainly seem a good fit with emerging evidence from the world of neuroscience, as we shall see in Chapter 3. Piaget suggested that children's curiosity drives their learning (Mooney 2000) and that through exploration and symbolic play, such as making an imaginary meal from pebbles, or playing spaceships in a cardboard box, they make sense of objects and the world.

Maria Montessori (1870–1952) also believed that children learn best through their senses, although not in a symbolic way. She argued that children have 'sensitive periods' when their senses are ready to learn new ideas and that if we spot these we can best support children's development. She suggested that children's senses come first in their intellect and that adults have a role to play in offering and arranging an interesting and attractive environment. She recognized the importance of providing appropriate materials and giving children adequate time and space to experiment, key roles that we will return to in Chapter 9.

Although Piaget and Montessori were key in promoting sensorial environments, interest in the senses started as early as the 1600s when John Comenius recommended sensory experiences rather than formal teaching for children. He is credited with introducing a visual focus to learning by adding illustrations to books. A transition can be seen as Friedrich Froebel (1782–1852) placed an emphasis upon sensory play and first-hand experience as a tool for learning, principles that were also reflected in his kindergarten. In the 1800s, Johann Pestalozzi emphasized the importance of the senses and basing learning on things that are familiar to children, a factor which we will return to throughout this book. Similarly, Rudolph Steiner (1861–1925) recognized that children learn from the people and environment that surround them, with Steiner settings characterized by natural open-ended materials that children can explore at their own pace, like the nature tables that many of us may have enjoyed at school.

Reggio Emilia pre-schools recognize the marriage between providing a quality environment and a supporting practitioner. The very design of space serves to maximize opportunities for sensory stimulation as children are able to gain 'an awareness of scale, colour, texture, sound, smell, light, microclimate' by virtue of the arrangement of space, use of mirrors, variety of transparency, reflectance, colour, texture and acoustic qualities that they encounter (Bishop 2001: 78). This exploration of different materials is further extended by the provision of stimulating resources and the use of professional artists and skilled practitioners whose role is to foster children's innate curiosity about the natural world, as partners rather than in a top-down approach. As early as the 1920s, Susan Isaacs saw the value of 'free, unfettered play' highlighting the role of the adult in supporting children to make sense of the world themselves. She recognized that 'no experimental scientist has a greater thirst for new facts than an ordinary, healthy, active child' (Pound 2006: 33), the roots of which lie in brain development, as we shall learn in Chapters 2 and 3. We will also see its manifestation in the trial and error investigations, so typical of heuristic and Treasure Basket play.

The outdoor environment and play

> Many of the ostensibly simple and commonplace phenomena which occur in nature and science are a source of wonderment and discovery to young children. The elements: rain, snow, mist, changes of season; how plants and animals grow; the nature of heat and cold; all provide opportunities for discovery, observation and wonder.
>
> (Geraghty 1990: 250)

Since much sensory play is freely available in the outdoor environment, synonymous itself with open-endedness, and noise and mess are less of a factor, it is worth introducing some of the pioneers of outdoor play. With a focus on health, Margaret McMillan's practice strongly encouraged play and rest outdoors, while Susan Isaacs recognized the benefits to exploration and enquiry from play outdoors. However, it was in 1995 that Forest Schools were established in the UK, with children being given the opportunity to explore woodland environments. Following the model established in Denmark, the Forest Schools movement has taken hold in the UK, capturing the hearts and minds of children and adults alike. The importance of the outdoor environment has also been reflected in evolving early years policy.

More recently the value of children accessing green spaces (the more natural the better) has been proved by a wealth of research demonstrating its health, emotional and behavioural benefits. Similarly, numerous studies have concluded that 'children's preferred environments include a predominance of natural elements' (Korpela 2002, cited in Evans and Wells 2003: 313) –

something that most parents and practitioners instinctively know. Positive benefits have been discovered just from looking at green views, let alone experiencing them first-hand (for example Kuo and Taylor 2004; Barton and Pretty 2010), and the idea of negative repercussions from lack of access to nature and the outdoor environment has been coined 'nature deficit disorder' (Louv 2005).

Improved attention helps children think more clearly, enabling them to respond better to the stresses of life. Attention Restoration Theory is suggested as a possible tool for understanding the restorative qualities of natural elements. This proposes that 'exposure to nature bolsters one's cognitive resources by allowing neural inhibitory mechanisms to rest and recover from use' (Evans and Wells 2003: 325). This recovery is believed to occur because of four characteristics closely associated with natural environments:

1   Fascination refers to nature's ability to effortlessly draw our attention and in doing so allow our brain to rest.
2   The sense of being away from daily worries provides a 'mental vacation'.
3   The extent of the environment gives ample opportunities to be immersed.
4   Finally, an environment which is compatible with a person's preferences, allows their attention to rest.

(Evans and Wells 2003: 325)

The 'physical characteristics of the home environment, such as the availability of toys and materials, a variety of stimulation, and adequate space for privacy and exploration, have been identified as potentially protective factors against the stresses of everyday life (Bradley *et al.* 1990, cited in Evans and Wells 2003: 315) and it seems plausible therefore for a Treasure Basket to provide restorative and buffering benefits that conventional plastic toys cannot.

A further factor to consider is the potential for a Treasure Basket to 'prime' children for fuller exploration and investigation of the natural environment. This idea emerged from a 'Forest Schools' session with 4- to 5-year-old children in the UK. While at the site, a sparsely wooded area on the edge of a school field, the adults and children were gathered in a log circle talking when the teacher asked the children to spend a few minutes thinking about their different senses. One at a time a talking stick was passed around the group and the children's comments struck me as being quick flowing, insightful and surprisingly sophisticated for their age. When I later commented on this to the teacher she explained that earlier that day they'd got the Treasure Basket out in the classroom to sit and talk about their senses, feeling the different objects as they did so. The experience of earlier that day and the opportunity to absorb and reflect may have contributed to the depth, speed and quality of the children's answers. The notion of a Treasure Basket being seen as a tool to help prepare children to get the most from the environment (definitely not as a replacement) is certainly worthy of further investigation.

Brain development

In the early 1990s, Brierley demonstrated the importance of pattern and variety in engaging the infant's brain (Brierley 1994). This still rings true but research has dramatically changed understanding since then. In particular it is now believed that although the early years remain a vital stage in brain development, the brain does not stop growing at 6 years of age; its 'plasticity' (ability to change) continues throughout our lives, peaking in infancy and adolescence. 'Sensitive periods' have replaced the emphasis upon 'critical windows' of development, in recognition of the brain's amazing ability to evolve (Howard-Jones 2007: 8). Broadly speaking, different parts of the brain are associated

Figure 1.1 Nature for the child is sheer sensory experience

with different functions and are responsible for processing different sensory information from the eyes, ears and other sensory organs. However, as we shall discover in Chapter 2, this does not happen in isolation and is far more fluid than previously believed. To make sense of the world the brain needs to sort and integrate all the different pieces of information in a complex process which most of us take for granted. The remainder of this chapter focuses on sensory-rich play generally, posing the questions 'What do experiences like play with a muddy puddle, tree roots or a Treasure Basket share?' and 'How can such sensory-rich experiences positively shape children's lives and learning?'

Children's responses to sensory play

Imagine a walk in the woods; a visit to the seaside; children mixing and splodging paint with a fat brush (better still, their fingers); or building with smooth wooden blocks. What do these all have in common? Each experience, like countless others, is inextricably linked to the senses. The woodland walk conjures up crunching leaves underfoot while dappled light is cast on tree trunks and the pungent smell of fungi pervades. A trip to the seaside offers the satisfaction of shaping wet sand, creating channels for frothing water and the taste of salty air. Painting gives the pleasure and cold silky feel of paint or the visual explosion of colour as shades mix and loop on an expanse of paper. Block play offers the opportunity to create imaginary castles with cool wooden blocks satisfyingly clinking as the creation takes shape. A beautiful Treasure Basket offers a veritable feast of sensory stimulation. The essence of all of these experiences is both captured and conveyed through the colour, sounds, feel, warmth, smells and taste of an infant's interaction. Children are typically hardwired to know how to 'do' sensory play and need no instructions when faced with sand, mud or water. Rather it is we adults who may have lost sight of the awe and wonder that such open-ended materials offer, the limitless possibilities and opportunities for quiet reflection, and the fact that some mess or even the momentary appearance of disorder (as children naturally choose to combine objects and resources) is definitely worth the effort. If the essential ingredients for nurturing quality play are the provision of space, time, materials and support this is all the more important when it comes to sensory play, given its immersive qualities.

Note: throughout the book a number of activities are suggested to help further our understanding in one or more of the following areas:

Environment

Adult 🖋

Child ☺

Activity 1

- Try to imagine a vivid childhood play memory.
- Was one or more of your senses really prominent? If yes, why do you think it is so vivid?
- How does the memory make you feel?
- Was an adult present?

As we will discover in Chapter 3, broad-based knowledge depends upon a multitude of separate multi-sensory actions, images and memories, developed and reshaped from a wealth of separate, yet interlinked experiences. When we hear the word 'forest' all our experiences relating to forests come to mind, from climbing trees and the satisfaction of balancing on a fallen log to feeling the texture of bark with fingertips, scrunching leaves, or feeling dappled light on the face. This is a multi-layered experience made up of sights, sounds, feelings and memories, like the memories of the rush of air on the face and scent of the forest while cycling through a wooded glade, the thrill of playing hide and seek or being chased, the exhilaration of swinging on a rope, or the coolness of a gurgling spring. Everybody will have their own unique set of 'mental files' based on their own interests and experiences as well as several in common. All these different sensory-rich experiences can potentially be accessed from the word 'forest' and will only come to life when encountered for oneself. No amount of stories and pictures will convey the essence or replace the magic of first-hand encounters as without the unique sensory experiences and memories that we attach to words, they lack resonance and meaning.

Activity 2

Imagine trying to describe snow to a visitor from another world for whom words have limited meaning.

- How difficult is it and how many different words do you need to use?
- How far from understanding the sensation do you think the visitor would be?
- Can you think of examples of when we tell a child something that they could discover better on their own?

Compare these sensory-rich experiences to the visual focus and passive nature of watching television or playing computer games – just two of the trends in twenty-first-century play cited in recent research (Gill 2011). Or visit the average toy shop, with shelf upon shelf of brightly coloured toys, some of which flash, bleep or talk, and the visual (and to a lesser extent auditory) focus of many toys is apparent. Opportunities for children to actually touch or taste are often discouraged, or restricted to plastic – limiting the creation of vivid memories. Being brought up in a plastic revolution we may unquestioningly accept or even embrace its contribution to life. However, as the visual stimulus of brightly coloured plastic toys is removed, their appeal and 'differentness' quickly disappears, reminding us of the sensory limitations of plastic as a toy, pacifier and feeding implement.

Activity 3

To gain infants' perspective on their largely plastic world try filling a bag with plastic toys.

- Close your eyes and place your hand in the bag of toys. What different 'sensations' (rather than objects) can you feel? Compare smells.
- Describe how it makes you feel, for example interested, excited, disinterested, bored?
- Are you surprised by the difference in quality experience between looking at and feeling the objects?
- Think about what words come to mind when you feel the toys. Contrast with your findings in **Activity 13**.

Modern play primarily takes place indoors, where temperatures are constant, and smells and environmental sounds masked. All this contributes to a sense-limiting experience, where opportunities for learning by doing are severely restricted. Contrast this with the vivid childhood play memories you may be lucky to have of 'running barefoot through grass', making 'mud pies' or 'rose petal perfume' and the appeal of multi-sensory play is evident (Papatheodorou 2010; Gill 2011). The natural environment appeals on many levels, as a constantly changing, full-bodied and open-ended instigator of play but also for the agency it offers children as they use nature's materials to create their own toys and games.

Tapping into this amazing connectivity, richness and immediacy of thought is essential to bringing any early years learning to life. As we shall discover in Chapter 7, the senses can help make learning relevant and real as well as fun! Crowe recognizes that

> without meaning words are useless ... words are connectors ...
> children's senses cry out to be used *first* to provide the experiences

that they will later need in order to connect. Children must feel their world, listen to it, see it, taste it, smell it, 'know' it . . . That takes time and a great deal of silent investigation in peace and privacy.

(Crowe 1983: 39)

We shall see these ideas in action later, in Chapters 5 and 6, as children explore simple objects with sand and water.

The benefits and features of sensory play

Throughout our lives sensory-rich experiences are vital for brain development. Neuroscientists have identified a strong link between memory recollections and the sense of sight, smell and touch. If you've ever encountered a particular smell, good or bad, that has brought memories flooding back, then you will have experienced this first-hand. Sensory-rich play is an inclusive way of encouraging learning and development, with the hands-on approach appealing to children with different thinking and learning styles. Sensory activities help bring learning to life and are great for children with English as an additional language and those who enjoy a practical approach, especially boys. But they need to be carefully tailored to support children with sensory processing difficulties. In a world in which our senses are bombarded, you don't have to look far to find sensory-rich play experiences. There are ample opportunities for engaging all the senses, through play outdoors, sand and water play, a Treasure Basket or other sensory-rich resources. All these activities also offer a multitude of other benefits that make them perfect for supporting children through any early years curriculum. Much of the beauty and appeal of sensory play resources lies in four characteristics: their simplicity, open-endedness, flexibility and relevance.

1 Simplicity

If you've ever commented on how children 'spend more time playing with the cardboard box than the present itself' then you will have witnessed some of the appeal and excitement of open-ended resources. When it comes to children's play, generally 'the simpler the resource, the better' as this leaves more scope for children to shift from 'What can this object do?' to 'What can I do with it?'

2 Open-endedness

One of the things I most enjoy about watching children playing with a Treasure Basket is that you never quite know what you will see. Creative examples of

Treasure Basket play will be shared in Chapter 7 as we explore how this simple resource can bring the curriculum to life, but it is fair to say that the open-ended nature of sensory-rich play (in that there are no 'right' or 'wrong' ways of playing) offers plentiful opportunities for developing children's skills in problem solving, exploration and creativity. The human brain thrives on variety, stimulation and the unexpected and, for children, play with sensory-rich resources offers just that. Open-ended materials, from a cardboard box to sand, paint, pebbles or a Treasure Basket, enable children (and adults) to represent their experiences, ideas and imagination. When as adults we look at an object like a pastry brush, we often see it for what it is, a brush, rather than a tickling stick, a paintbrush, microphone or mini broom. Children's thinking tends to be less rigid so every natural treasure in the environment or in a Treasure Basket has the potential to be whatever a child wants it to be.

Young children do not have a monopoly on using natural resources or their imagination to conjure up role-play. Older children will delight in creating intricate 'fairy meals' using acorn cups for bowls, creating rose petal perfume or lavender wine, engineering a toxic sludge, witch's potion, hearty 'stews' or cement for construction from mud, sand, twigs, water and so on. With access to a few simple household objects like saucepans, pots, whisks and spoons, recycled containers, twigs, leaves, seedpods and other natural treasures found outdoors, children's creativity and imagination can have a free rein. Of course this will only be the case if they are given the time, space and permission to do so.

3 Flexibility

Sensory-rich play resources are found all around us and most children do not need any help in signposting these, nor any instructions on what to do to maximize their play potential! In one play session a group of children (aged 2–8 years) added biodegradable, loose-fill 'peanuts' (similar to polystyrene packing pieces) to water, discovering that when wet they disintegrate to create very realistic effluent scum! Another child spotted the packaging and a small tin and proceeded to see how many pieces he could fit in the tin. He paused several times, explaining that it was full, before devising another strategy to create more space, be it putting the tin lid on to press the pieces down, squeezing them with his fingers, or putting the tin on the floor so he could press down with more force. Once full, he announced that he wanted to count them to see how many he'd squeezed in and therefore set about emptying the tin. This required another strategy as many of the pieces had stuck together, so a spoon was needed to prise them out when his finger could no longer reach them. Another child, aged 8, excitedly called out 'Look!' as she held up a creation for the other children to see. The subject of excitement and pride was some packaging pieces that she had rolled in sand

and couscous to create a look-a-like cheesy nibble! The other children looked on with awe and wonder before a flurry of hands began scooping up packaging pieces to use in their own play. As this example illustrates, with the right context it's easy for simple yet highly sensory resources to spark creativity and play in children of all ages.

4 Relevance

Key to a successful Treasure Basket is selecting objects that are culturally relevant. A Treasure Basket can cross boundaries to enhance the context and content of a child's culture. 'A well-stocked basket with carefully selected objects can give babies the opportunities to explore those things that make up their world' (Forbes 2004: 17). Not only can a collection of objects better reflect the community of interest in which they are created but, unlike many manufactured toys, they are culturally appropriate. Roopnarine *et al.* (1998, cited in Hughes 2003) point to the inherent contradiction of branded toys, like Barbie, being offered in communities where their values and culture are at odds. It is difficult to see the significance of such licensed toys to children's play and lives, and these may actually help erode societal values. The 'term "toy" is often given to things that adults have designed or selected specifically to engage a child, but fascination with the properties of things extends to many other objects as well' (Garvey 1986: 44), as we shall discover.

These four characteristics of sensory-rich play also flag up areas to consider when planning for children's individual needs. What is simple or relevant for one child may not be for another. Ultimately the balance between the environment, children's needs and adults' actions will determine what this looks like in practice, making this a useful appraisal tool. The Sensory Play Continuum, summarized in Table 1.1, brings together these three dimensions, providing an appropriate environment by:

- offering different options at the three stages;
- meeting the child's needs in terms of picking activities and resources, and offering them in different ways to support their needs; and
- getting the adult/child balance right.

I developed the Continuum as a framework for extending the use of Treasure Baskets with older children and children with SEN (Gascoyne 2009). By placing sensory play and the senses at its heart, the Continuum ensures an emphasis upon the often forgotten sensory dimension of play. The three Continuum stages are based upon actual observations of play with a Treasure Basket and help adults achieve the optimum balance between adult-led and child-led play as recommended in the EPPE report (Sylva *et al.* 2004), as we will explore further in Chapters 5 and 6. Although presented as distinct and sequential stages, this is to oversimplify the process which can flow seamlessly from one stage to another in an iterative cycle as well as being accessed in a different order, as we shall discover in Chapter 9.

As this brief skim through the key shapers in sensory play has revealed, the value of sensory-rich experiences has long featured as an undercurrent of play theory. Sensory-rich play holds a fascination for children and is freely available in the outdoor environment, sharing numerous characteristics and benefits with a Treasure Basket. Although the adult's role may not be obvious in the first two stages of the Continuum, it is nevertheless essential for providing an appropriately stimulating environment, understanding the needs of children, and recognizing adults' own sensory preferences (Gascoyne 2011).

We will return to the interplay between these in Chapter 9. Understanding the sensory domain is key to illuminating children's needs, so we will now explore the senses, the gateway and foundation for all learning.

Table 1.1 The Sensory Play Continuum

Continuum stage	Type of play	Features
Stage 1	**Free play**	Babies and children play freely with the resources without any adult involvement.
Stage 2	**Combining resources**	The Treasure Basket is offered next to another resource such as sand, water, magnets or mirrors, to further extend its appeal and play potential. Children play freely although if appropriate the adult *responds* to the child's questions.
Stage 3	**Adult-initiated play**	The final stage of the Continuum involves using simple adult-initiated activities with Treasure Basket objects, like guessing whether objects will sink or float in water. Activities may be inspired by children themselves.

2 Our amazing senses

All of us process sensory input 24 hours a day, starting from the moment we are born. It is the integration of this sensory information that shapes our perceptions, defines our realities and drives our behaviours

(Emmons and Anderson, *Understanding Sensory Dysfunction*)

Overview

This chapter sets out the vital role played by our external and lesser known internal senses, exploring how each of these operates and their complex relationship to the brain. Drawing upon contemporary research and a literature review to provide the latest perspective on the ever-changing field of neuroscience, each of the senses will be introduced as a precursor to focusing on sensory processing. Throughout the chapter, practical examples and activities help make the link between our senses and early childhood theory and practice.

Although often taken for granted, it is scarcely imaginable for us to think about life without our senses. Using the analogy of an unlit house with solid metal walls and roof we can picture our external sense organs as the windows through which we discover the world and ourselves, and our internal senses as the valves and switches controlling inside. With no contact with the outside world and none of these controls, it would be like having no sense organs to know what is happening within and around us (Riedman 1962). The importance of sensory-rich experiences cannot be overemphasized in providing the source of all learning and enrichment in our daily lives. To give a better understanding, this chapter introduces the brain and each of the senses, explaining how they work and their particular role in decoding objects, the foundation for learning.

The brain

The cerebral cortex is the softly folded, walnut-like outer surface of the brain that many of us will picture when we hear the word 'brain'. The cortex, formed from about 10 million neurons (or brain cells), is divided into two distinct halves, the left and right hemispheres, which give it its distinct wrinkled appearance. The left side primarily focuses on speech and movement and the right on visual patterns, but this is to oversimplify its complexity. The two sides of the brain are connected by the corpus callosum, a thick band of nerves which enables the two halves to work in perfect harmony. To complicate things further, most sensory information crosses from one side of the brain to the other to be analysed.

Each hemisphere has four lobes: the temporal (associated with memory and auditory skills); occipital at the rear of the head (responsible for visual processing); parietal (associated with integrating information and mathematical skills); and frontal lobe (the area behind the forehead associated with cognitive thinking and movement). In addition, different parts of the cortex are 'specialized' for hearing, taste, smell, touch, sight and movement. Beneath the cortex at the rear of the head lies the cerebellum. This deeply ridged area is described by Brierley (1994: 14) as the 'automatic pilot'. It is responsible for habituated actions, things that once learnt we don't need to think about, like walking, handwriting, or riding a bike. Deep within the brain is the limbic system including the thalamus – the central 'switchboard' for receiving and analysing all sensations.

The senses

Given the Treasure Basket's origins in the sensory domain it is fitting to set this discussion within the context of our senses. All learning in life ultimately stems from the senses, an amazingly sophisticated system for receiving and decoding information. As we will discover later in this chapter, rather than the five senses instilled in us as children, which has its origins in Aristotle, according to Smith (1984), there are in fact at least six senses vital to everyday life. Although the commonly cited external senses are vital, the lesser-known but crucially important inner or 'sixth' senses detect position, balance, movement and more – see Table 2.1. Similarly, when we think of our senses, our eyes, ears and nose spring to mind, but really our whole body is a sensory organ as the skin, and our internal sense organs like the inner ear, are packed with receptors to detect touch, pressure, heat, cold and pain. When working effectively, we are oblivious to the complexity of the process; it is only when sensory processing difficulties arise (as

Table 2.1 The senses

External Senses	Internal (6th) senses
Visual (sight)	Vestibular (balance)
Olfactory (smell)	Proprioceptive (position in space)
Auditory (sound)	Kinaesthetic (movement)
Tactile (touch)	Baric (weight)
Gustatory (taste)	Thermic (temperature)

detailed in Chapter 8) that the miracle of the brain's workings are fully appreciated.

Processing sensory information

Every sensory experience provides the foundations upon which all subsequent knowledge, thought and creativity are based. Clearly we do not live in a one-dimensional sensory world so our senses do not operate in isolation. On a simplistic level, each time an individual encounters a sensory stimulus a neuron (brain cell) connects to another neuron, establishing new connections in the brain. Signals flow along these complex neural networks, from one neuron to another, allowing the brain cells to communicate with each other by relaying information about emotions as well as everything we see, hear, taste, touch and smell. Each new sensory stimulus adds to the network, while repeated experiences increase the thickness and strength of the connections, helping signals to travel faster and more efficiently (Carlson-Finnerty and Wartik 1993). In this way each of us will develop a unique network of nerve connections created from our own unique sensory experiences, which means that 'the richer our sensory experiences the more intricate will be the patterns for learning, thought and creativity' (Hannaford 1995: 30). In reality, each sense works in its own unique way, so it is helpful to focus on the individual senses in order to understand better the complex processes at play. Starting with the external senses, most developed at birth, we will begin our tour.

Olfactory – smell

The sense of smell is one of our most underused senses and yet, together with the sense of touch, it is the most developed at birth. Not surprisingly perhaps, smell and touch (both linked to the oldest limbic part of the brain) are very strongly associated with childhood memories and emotion. Forbes and

Butterworth each cite research by MacFarlane in 1975 carried out at the John Radcliffe Maternity Unit where breast milk was soaked onto pads and the babies responded only to their mother's milk, by turning their head towards the familiar scent (cited in Butterworth and Harris 1994 and Forbes 2004). In other research a child vividly recalled the smell of freshly curled wood shavings from her grandfather's workshop and warmly associated the smell of wood with happy times playing with 'Granddad's coffins' – he was a coffin-maker (Papatheodorou 2010)! Crowe reflects upon how older people vividly recalled the smell of paraffin lamps, medicine chests, carbolic soap, cooking, DIY, and 'wash-day' smells. But with extractor fans, air fresheners, convenience foods and washing appliances 'so many distinctive smells that children could read like a book, connecting them with people, homes and seasons, have been removed or replaced by synthetics' (Crowe 1983: 36).

Our smell receptors are located in our nostrils and, unlike all the other senses, feedback from these does not cross hemispheres, so a smell sensed in the left nostril travels to the left side of the brain. Free-flowing air currents carry odours to the nose, but when we sniff this creates stronger currents, able to pull more odour molecules into the nose and up to the receptors in the nasal cavities. There the nasal mucosa – hairy, tentacle-like receptors – wave in the current, absorbing the odour and sending an impulse to the olfactory tract (Bogdashina 2003). We typically 'tune out' most smells other than those that are either delicious or disgusting but, as we shall discover in Chapter 8, for some children hypersensitive to smell, concentration on anything can be difficult, being bombarded as they are by offensive smells. Other children may try to sniff everything in their quest for stimulation.

It's hard to imagine, but our nose contains about 10 million smell receptors made up of 20 various types, each responsible for detecting a different type of smell (Bogdashina 2003). Impressive as that sounds, humans are considered the 'poor cousins' of other mammals in the olfactory world, with dogs' sense of smell 'one million times better than man' (Smith 1984: 186). The sense of smell is inextricably linked to the sense of taste, as we are all too aware of when we have a blocked nose and food tastes nondescript or bland. The part of the brain responsible for analysing taste and smell, called the olfactory bulb and tract, is located adjacent to the hippocampus in the brain, which is responsible for memory. From an evolutionary perspective, a good memory of unpleasant – and therefore potentially dangerous – things was a key aspect of survival. Nowadays, supermarkets exploit the importance of smell in their stores, piping the intoxicating aroma of freshly baked bread towards the entrances. Estate agents describe the value of freshly brewed coffee to encourage property viewers into a positive and aspirational frame of mind, yet we use our sense of smell less and less, scarcely giving consideration to the importance of stimulating this sense in everyday childcare provision.

Activity 4

As one of our most underused senses it is important for us to provide opportunities for stimulating the sense of smell. Try these activities with babies and children.

- Gather some clean odd socks or mini organza bags, cotton wool pads and a range of different herbs, spices, flavoured oils and smelly substances like coffee, fruit tea leaves, vanilla pods, lavender and cinnamon sticks. **Always check allergies first.** Put a little of each smelly item in a sock or bag (for the liquids add drops to the cotton wool instead). Tie the socks/bags securely with ribbon or string before offering to babies and children to smell. With babies introduce each smell one at a time to avoid sensory overload and to understand more about their likes and dislikes. Do so by gently stroking their legs, toes or arms, so that the smell slowly wafts to their nose. Let the baby discover the smell and watch closely to see their reaction. If appropriate, talk about each smell as the baby explores. Take it in turns smelling and accentuate reactions – 'Mmm that smells lovely', or 'Aarggh, that's pongy'.
- Invite older children to guess what each smell is, possibly by matching word or picture cards to each smell. Use to inspire smelly stories or games. Open up the socks/bags to discover what each smell 'looks like'. Talk about what they are, where they come from, how they're used, what they like or dislike and if they remind them of anything.
- Offer a selection of smelly substances/foods for older children to explore smelly art or collage. Coffee, fruit tea bags and normal tea could work well.

Although a carefully conceived Treasure Basket should appeal to the sense of smell through the inclusion of leather, metal, lavender and dried whole fruit, for example, children are rarely seen simply smelling the objects, although of course this will happen while mouthing. Scientists believe that the proximity of smell and memory receptors is not the only factor at play in the vivid, smell-induced memories that we experience. The smell itself is believed to act as a highly effective 'retrieval cue' when testing adults' memories, much like the visual and auditory cues that we all possess (Engan and Ross 1973, cited in Moxon 2000: 36).

Activity 5

When selecting items for a Treasure Basket be sure to think about the sense of smell and select items that will particularly appeal to this, e.g. metal, leather, a shell, lavender bag, fresh lemon, lime or orange – pricked first with a fork. **Avoid keys as these may be toxic.**

Tactile – touch

Typically, children's lives include plentiful visual experiences while tactile experiences are more limited. 'We are reminded of the multi-sensory synchronicity of the brain by the notion of "children's exploring fingers [as] an extension of their eyes"' (Brierley 1993, cited in Broadhead 2004: 7). Our skin is the sensory organ responsible for the sense of touch – one of the first senses to develop, even before birth. Within the layers of skin five different types of receptors are located to detect pressure, heat, cold, pain and light touch. Some of these are found just beneath the outer dead layer of the epidermis, while others are found deep within the dermis layer of the skin. Touch receptors are not evenly distributed across the body, with the majority located in the mouth, lips and hands. The importance of the mouth and hands becomes apparent when watching a young baby playing with a Treasure Basket. Most objects accidentally, then purposefully selected will ultimately end up being mouthed, this being the area in which most touch receptors are located. Similarly, when older children encounter an unfamiliar object and usual investigation sheds little light, they may mouth the object to try to discover what it is.

Crucial to everyday life is what Ayres described as 'habituation', when a feeling or sensation fades and becomes accepted as a habit (Ayres 1972). For most of us the sensation of wearing clothes quickly fades after we get dressed. For some children with sensory processing difficulties, habituation does not occur and these sensations continue to have an invasive sensory presence in everyday life, bombarding and overwhelming them. If you've ever been irritated by a label in an item of clothing then try to imagine what it might be like to be constantly aware of everything you touch.

Activity 6

For many young children the home can present a multitude of opportunities to touch and explore and yet many of these may be discouraged and forbidden (some rightly so for safety reasons). In these crucial early years it is vital for babies and young children to be given ample opportunities to experience the world through touch. Offer a Treasure Basket for children to discover a world in a basket (see Chapter 4 for guidance).

Understanding infants' sense of touch

Few infants can resist the urge to mouth objects yet this is not universally welcomed by adults. Like the grandmother seen following her granddaughter around the room trying to remove the tightly clasped item that she was mouthing, some adults find it difficult to accept mouthing for a host of possible reasons, many understandable. As well as being entirely natural behaviour, it makes sense, this being one of the most sensitive parts of the infant's body. Just how sensitive the mouth is, and how much children can learn from mouthing is perhaps misunderstood.

Butterworth and Harris cite Meltzoff and Barton's experiments in the 1970s revealing a staggeringly sophisticated sense of touch in babies aged just 29 days old. Two groups of babies were given a different shaped pacifier to suck. One group received a conventionally smooth dummy while the other had a dummy with nodules on the teet. Neither group of babies actually saw what they were sucking. The babies were then shown two large-scale models of both dummies. Babies were found to fixate on the model that was the same shape as the dummy they had sucked for 70 per cent of the total fixation time (1994). These findings are noteworthy as they show that not only does oral exploration convey information to a baby about what an object looks like, but at just 1 month of age the sense of touch and vision appear to be working in unison so that 'infants can recognise the equivalence of information picked up by different sensory modalities' (Butterworth and Harris 1994: 68). This is hugely significant to our understanding of the importance of mouthing generally and specifically in terms of Treasure Basket play. Through mouthing and exploring the Treasure Basket objects with their fingers and mouth, children are able to gain multi-sensory feedback and develop a much better grasp of the world around them.

We know that the hands are disproportionately sensitive and geared up to detect sensory feedback. Add to this the degree of control that we typically have over our fingers and thumbs, in terms of position, direction and amount of pressure, and the importance of our hands as explorative tools becomes clear. 'We have evolved sophisticated processes for exploring the environment and objects using touch in very exact and careful ways' (Brace and Pike 2005: 118). If functioning effectively, a feedback system relays information from the touch receptors in the fingers and thumbs to the brain and this in turn regulates the precise location and amount of pressure being applied. In this way simply by touching an object we know the exact location of the fingers (from kinaesthetic and proprioceptive information) and what the object feels like (from touch receptor information). This combination of different information, known as 'haptic information', helps us understand and describe objects. It is also believed that young children's concept of weight is significantly influenced by the felt weight of an object. According to research it is only at around 9 years of age that 'children develop a concept of weight that is less dependent on their personal sensations' (cited in Wilkening and Huber 2002: 364).

Lederman and Klatzky (1987: 345) discovered a series of exploratory procedures typically seen in adults when they use their hands to explore objects. Further investigation of these revealed a link between how the object was explored and the information elicited, with people typically moving their fingers around an object's contours to subconsciously elicit information about the object's shape. If, however, the focus is determining firmness, the exploratory procedure typically seen was fingers pressing the object. Six different types of movement were identified, each of which are attributed to a different type of information generated through exploration (see Table 2.2).

Figure 2.1 Exploring treasures is an all-encompassing experience

Table 2.2 Taxonomy of exploratory hand procedures

Movement	Information	Object properties		Hierarchy
Enclose object in hand(s)	Overall shape	Geometric properties	Material properties	1
Following contours with fingers	More exact shape	Size and shape		2
Lateral motion with fingers	Texture		Texture (including roughness and stickiness), spatial density, hardness, temperature, weight	3
Press with fingers	Hardness			
Static contact with fingers	Temperature			
Unsupported holding	Weight			

Source: Adapted from Lederman and Klatzky 1987: 345, Table 1 and Klatzky and Lederman 2002: 154

Although much of this is common sense, research does not yet extend to exploring if and when these behaviours begin to emerge in children. Observations of Treasure Basket play reveal an array of fine manipulative skills in action during exploration. We know that the hands are disproportionately sensitive to stimulation and that during infancy children's experiences are shaping their understanding of the world. Research has discovered the importance of hand and finger position for infants in interpreting other people's behaviour. For example, an adult making a grasping action appears to be interpreted by even very young children as a goal-orientated action (rather than random movement), based on the infant's transference of their own motives when making the same action. Similarly Liben (1999, cited in Liben 2002: 336) found that infants 'adjust their grasping movements in ways that suggest that they have extracted spatial (shape) features of the objects'. With this in mind it is suggested that the sort of manipulative actions typically seen during Treasure Basket play may be linked to a complex process of rule acquisition, categorization and developing mental files rather than simply exploration *per se*. If the basis for Lederman and Klatzky's exploratory processes lies in the type of fine manipulative skills typically seen in infants' handling of objects, then this would infer far greater importance to this aspect of Treasure Basket play than previously considered.

Activity 7

Observe children of different ages playing with a Treasure Basket. Notice how they use their hands to touch the objects. Try with a group of adults (without disclosing what you are observing). Plot the objects and different hand positions on a grid and compare and contrast with the exploratory procedures in Table 2.2. Reflect upon your findings with other practitioners and parents.

Visual – sight

Although not the most developed sense at birth, our visual sense is the most stimulated sense, with 80 per cent of all stimulation in the environment visual. This makes it probably the most important of the external senses. Our brains are hardwired to search for pattern and variety, and yet take away the bright colours from most plastic toys and, unless they have added sounds, children are offered very little in the way of sensory appeal. Babies' brains are programmed to recognize complex patterns like the features of a face or geometric patterns, something even newborn babies can do. Although not fully developed, the newborn's eyes are ingeniously 'programmed' to focus best at an adult arm's length, the distance between a carer's face and a feeding baby. According to Hamer, this does not mean that infants cannot focus at other distances. They can, but with more limited control and haphazard focusing (Hamer 1990).

When we think of the sense of sight, our eyes are the obvious sensory organ, but in fact without the sophisticated processes at work in the brain we would effectively be blind. The visual system is made up of three distinct elements:

1 the organs of sight, i.e. the eyes;
2 the optic nerves which transmit visual images from the eye and transport it to the brain; and
3 the visual cortex, the part of the brain responsible for interpreting the information received from the optic nerves.

If a problem occurs in any of these three elements of the visual system, it can impact upon a child's ability to see. Although distinct, these three parts are also interdependent, so that a problem in one part of the system will impact upon another.

1 The eyes

Our eyes are the sense organ responsible for vision and their function is to receive and channel light into the nerve endings in the retina at the back of the eye. In many ways the eye works much like a camera. Each eye has a convex lens to help aim and focus images and an iris (the coloured ring) controlling the amount of light entering the eye, by enlarging or decreasing the size of the pupil (the black centre). The iris opens to allow more light in and, conversely, in bright conditions it closes, reducing the size of the pupil. Light passes through the cornea, covering the iris, projecting through the lens behind the pupil. The lens focuses light through the jelly-like vitreous humour onto the back of the inner eye. This happens through a process called accommodation, as the muscles attached to the lens change its shape to enable the eye to focus. This ability to adjust to focus on a near or far object works best in childhood.

The retina records the image upside down and reversed before transmitting this image through the optic nerves to the brain to be interpreted. As each eye covers a slightly different visual field and sees objects from a different angle, the brain also has the task of combining the images and making sense of them, including filling any missing gaps. Vital for everyday functioning, this can also be responsible for so-called 'optical illusions'. The sensory information then passes to the visual processing part of the brain, located at the back of the head, where different types of information, like colour, shape, size, distance, movement, detail and peripheral vision (from the rods and cones in the retina) are analysed by different parts of the brain. Each eye is held in place by six extra-ocular muscles allowing movement as well as ensuring that both eyes work together to provide binocular vision. A problem with alignment will seriously impact on vision and life skills as the brain will struggle to piece together the images from both eyes (Kurtz 2006).

2 The optic nerve

An optic nerve projects from behind the retina in each eye to take visual information to the brain. Before the optic nerves enter the brain some of the fibres from each optic nerve cross to the opposite side of a structure called the optic chiasm. In this way each optic nerve travelling to the brain contains fibres which project images from both eyes and information from each eye is sent to both sides of the brain. This explains why, with a loss of sight in one eye, images from both eyes will still be conveyed to the brain or damage to either optic nerve may affect vision in both hemispheres (Kurtz 2006).

3 The visual cortex

When both optic nerves reach the visual cortex in the occipital lobe of the brain they project images onto their respective hemisphere. It is here that visual information is decoded and conveyed to the temporal and parietal lobes of the brain to be interpreted. With a better understanding of the plasticity of the brain, focus has shifted from 'critical' to 'sensitive' times, recognizing that the brain continues growing, albeit at a lesser pace, throughout adulthood. Characterized by a remarkable ability to adapt in the event of illness, injury or changes in environmental or emotional context, different parts of the brain can evolve to fulfil functions of other parts of the brain. However, early diagnosis of visual (and auditory) processing problems and treatment, such as an eye patch for a lazy eye, or corneal or cochlea implant, will greatly increase children's chances of being able to see or hear fully.

So sophisticated are the workings of the brain that true analogies are simplistic and flawed, but like the example of a digital camera, with a memory card packed with vivid images, it is only when plugged into a computer hard-drive that those images come to life. Similarly, with careful editing, the image can be cropped, air brushed and moulded, just as the brain fills the gaps in the sensory information provided by the eyes to create the final image that we see. Parallels can also be drawn in how the images are stored and retrieved. As we will discover in Chapter 3, each word or image ultimately links to a wealth of sensory-rich experiences that we readily retrieve through association and memory. Similarly a system for archiving the gigabytes of images that many of us accrue is crucial to their rapid retrieval!

Activity 8

While walking the dog one afternoon at dusk I was struck by the presence of something different. A cloud formation had created a 'Himalayan landscape' on the horizon, complete with snow-capped peaks. I rushed back to get my 5- and 8-year-olds who stood marvelling at the 'landscape' and how the play of light looked like snow. It is small experiences like these as well as fun visualizing activities which increase interconnectivity in the brain and reinforce the connections associated with sight. They are also great for forging visual memories.

• Maximize hands-on, memory-making opportunities for learning, particularly those created by natural phenomena. Try to look at the world with child-like eyes to see its awe and wonder so you can convey this to children too.

- Invite children to imagine they are playing at the seaside/in the wood and to think about the sorts of sights, sounds and smells they might experience.

Understanding infants' sense of vision

Although anatomically fully formed, the visual system of newborns still needs to mature (Kurtz 2006). At birth they will be able to detect light, dark and pattern, and a reflex closes their eyes in bright light. Research has also shown infants' preference for complex patterns such as the features that make up a face. As connections in the brain develop, with time these are myelinated (or insulated) to enable electrical signals to pass from one neuron to another quicker and more efficiently. The nerve fibres carrying information from the eyes and skin are myelinated first, enabling an infant to engage in sensory-rich explorative play, essential for promoting further brain development. This clever timing ensures that the other senses are developed before children try to take their first steps.

According to Kurtz (2006), infants are more attracted to the edges or boundaries of visual patterns than the internal portions of patterns. By about 3 to 4 months, infants show interest in all of the patterns, not just the edges, and are better able to track moving targets, adjust focus as objects move towards or away from them, and control eye movements so that both eyes move together in binocular vision. These skills are a necessary precursor to developing hand–eye co-ordination, so it is no coincidence that by the age of 3 to 4 months infants begin to reach purposefully for objects, as their accuracy of vision, eye movements and hand–eye co-ordination synchronize.

> As the baby begins to see and to manipulate objects within reach, visual input becomes closely associated with the tactile input to develop an inner language of basic concepts, such as hardness/softness, heavy/light, and round/square. The infant develops an awareness of these basic concepts long before he or she has the language to express an understanding of these concepts. This is the beginning of early visual perceptual development, especially the perception of form, shape, colour, size and other simple attributes.
>
> (Kurtz 2006: 22)

Although infants will not see colours in their full glory or distinguish between subtle shades until they are about 4 months old, by 8 or 9 weeks of age, a baby will be able to distinguish between two shades of grey, differing in brightness by just 0.5 per cent (Hamer 1990). By 5–7 months, co-ordination of the eyes has improved, enabling infants to judge distances better as well as spatial relationships to objects. This, suggests Kurtz (2006: 22) 'underlies the development of gross and fine motor skills as the infant moves within the environment and contacts objects based on perceptual judgement of their location'. By the age of 6 months binocular vision prevails, adding depth to infants' visual image. Accordingly infants become more interested in looking at three- rather than two-dimensional objects (Kurtz 2006), which explains in part some of the appeal of a Treasure Basket of objects.

In a label-less world it is easy to forget that an infant needs to discover that a living animal is fundamentally different to an inanimate object. Research has revealed how children as young as 3–4 months can distinguish between animals and furniture. What's more, within these categories, they can also distinguish between cats, dogs, chairs, beds and so on, with the animacy of objects a key appeal for infants (Sims 2006). Another factor, often overlooked, is the challenge of understanding that an object looks different when viewed from different angles. This explains why young children find 'posting' toys so difficult as not only do they need to recognize an object's shape (let alone capital letters) from different viewpoints, but if they manage to find the correct piece and post it, they are unable to recheck this to cement learning, as the piece has disappeared from view. Again, a Treasure Basket brimming full of objects is a perfect test-bed for perfecting these skills, without any pressure to perform or solve a problem set by someone else. By 18 months, hand and eye movements are closely integrated and, due to a combination of visual and motor memory, familiar tasks like walking or hand movements are no longer reliant on the eyes watching to guide them Kurtz (2006).

Gustatory – taste

Our tastebuds or receptors are located on the tongue, roof of the mouth and the inside of our cheeks. These are responsible for detecting sweet, salty, sour, bitter and the more recently acknowledged brothy taste called 'umami'. Taste is largely determined by feedback from smell and touch, with texture inextricably linked to the whole flavour sensation.

Activity 9

Cut up different types of fruit for children to taste. With weaning babies every new food encountered is a sensory adventure, so offer a range of different foods (one at a time initially) in order to maximize sensory interest. Older children can match tastes and fruit to words or pictures. Use common and exotic fruits and offer the whole fruit to see and feel as well as tasting bite-sized pieces. Talk about the taste, what it is, whether they like it, what it reminds them of (if anything) and where it grows. All of these will help increase the connections in their brain associated with that particular fruit. **Check allergies first.**

Although recollections of taste tend to feature least in our memories, most adults can recall the special taste of fresh bread, a leather strap, plasticine or coins. Indeed, as we've already discussed in exploring the sense of touch, infants typically mouth objects. Crowe concurs:

> A perfectly natural part of our play was to put things in our mouths, and [a] perfectly natural part of our learning was discovering what tasted like what, and whether we liked it. Sometimes we liked the feel but not the flavour, sometimes neither, and sometimes the flavour was harmless but the feel revolting.
>
> (Crowe 1983: 36)

I have observed very few children who enjoy mouthing objects with a very strong taste such as a lavender sachet in a Treasure Basket, and several who have responded with obvious surprise and disgust having tried!

Understanding infants' sense of taste

Babies develop their sense of taste while still in the womb. It is believed that the tastes which reoccur frequently in the womb become registered in the baby's memory in the same way that visual memories do. Like adults, newborn babies have a dislike of sour taste and can discriminate between sweet (pleasant) and sour (unpleasant) tastes when just a few hours old with no oral experience of food (Steiner 1979, cited in Butterworth and Harris 1994: 55). Like smell this may originate in survival tactics, with sour associated with poison and danger.

Auditory – hearing

Our ears are responsible for receiving auditory information but the inner ear also contains the semi-circular canals responsible for the vestibular system – the sense of gravity and balance. With hearing in the typically developed child near perfect at birth, the ear is divided into three parts: the inner, middle and outer ear. The external outer ear directs sound waves into the auditory canal from where they travel to the eardrum. A series of vibrations continue to the hammer, anvil and stirrup of the middle ear, which in turn cause the membrane between the middle and fluid-filled inner ear to vibrate. This sends electrochemical information through the thalamus to the auditory cortex for processing. Like most of our senses, this sound information is processed in the auditory cortex of the opposite hemisphere of the brain to the ear which receives it (Bogdashina 2003).

Activity 10

Offer a range of resources which are not musical instruments for spontaneous music-making, e.g. seeds or gravel in homemade shakers, containers covered with fabric to make drums, spoons and saucepans, bubble wrap and junk-modelling materials. Explore pitch, rhythm, tempo etc. **Supervise play at all times**.

Understanding infants' sense of hearing

From birth, babies' senses are primed to detect touch, space, their mother's smell, voice and repeated sounds. Hughes gives the example of a baby already accustomed to the theme tune of *Coronation Street* from exposure in the womb. On hearing it as a newborn, the baby turned towards the sound and 'suddenly became alert and responsive' (Hughes 2006: 18). Another study in 1984 reinforces our understanding of foetus's ability to hear while still in the womb. De Casper and Fifer asked 16 pregnant women to read aloud *The Cat in the Hat* by Dr Seuss twice a day for the last six-and-a-half weeks of pregnancy. When the babies were later tested using a special dummy connected to tape recordings of their mother's voice, a preference was apparent for the recording of the story that they had been exposed to in the womb, as opposed to another story which they had not previously heard (adapted from *Science* 1984: 225, 302–3, cited in Moxon 2000: 1). Not only does this reveal that babies' hearing is well developed even before birth, but it also shows that unborn babies are able to remember uterine experiences.

This knowledge of babies' memory-making potential is a powerful reminder of the wonder of the brain and the importance of babies being offered sensory-rich experiences, rather than this being left to children 3 years of age and above. I can still recall visiting nurseries to arrange childcare for my first child, when she was just 9 months old. I was shocked to discover just how varied the provision was, particularly for the youngest of children. Time after time I was told by a kindly practitioner that 'we don't do much in the baby room apart from give lots of cuddles as they are just babies'. Instinctively, I felt this was wrong and happily discovered a setting that shared my views. In the intervening years, numerous training initiatives have been developed for staff working with babies in response to our increasing understanding of the scales of development taking place in the first months and years of life. Far from painting the picture of babies as helpless, incomplete 'vessels to fill', we now understand so much more about the wonder of babies' brains.

Crowe refers to the nostalgic qualities of auditory memories like 'Mother's wedding ring clinking against the side of a pastry bowl' (Crowe 1983: 37). Worryingly, younger generations' memories are less closely linked to sounds, dulled perhaps by increasingly invasive background sounds, and the interactive dimension of many toys. This has important implications for memory-making and retrieval.

Activity 11

Introduce plentiful opportunities for listening to sounds in the natural environment, from birds to planes to silence. When raining, shelter under tarpaulins or umbrellas to experience the sound and vibrations first hand and forge children's memories.

Vestibular, proprioception and kinaesthetic

Our lesser-known vestibular, proprioceptive and kinaesthetic senses are responsible for relaying information about gravity and motion (vestibular), position in space (proprioceptive) and muscular movement (kinaesthetic). Without these vital inner senses, children would not be able to achieve fundamental milestones like taking their first steps, as these senses pass messages to the brain about movement, balance and changes in the position of the head. The vestibular system controls balance and movement with most of its sensory organs found in the ears. The cutaneous system, in the skin, receives sensory input for force, enabling us to grasp objects with just the right amount of force to hold but not crush. The kinaesthetic system receives movement information from receptors in the body's muscles, joints and tendons. It is amazing to consider that in little over one year, most children develop from reflex movements at birth to being able to stand, walk and even run. Many of children's full-bodied actions require balance and are dependent upon the development of these inner senses. For most of us our only reminder of these senses is a bout of travel sickness or feeling dizzy after a spin on a merry-go-round (Hannaford 1995). For children with proprioceptive difficulties, they are reliant on constant feedback, from movement or fidgeting, to reaffirm their position in space. Instead of being able to focus on the story that is being read or the ball that they need to catch, they also need to attend to feedback about their position and movement.

Sensory processing

Historically, neuroscience has tended to focus on the different sensory modalities of vision, taste, touch and so on, or even the sub-modalities of colour or depth perception (if concentrating on vision). While a focus on the individual senses adds to our understanding, neuroscientists now 'realise that real world experiences are multi-sensory in nature, and thus studying how the senses interact is essential' (Miller *et al.* 2009: 6). Now that each of the senses have been individually explored it is essential to put these in a multi-sensory context.

Although these systems develop largely independently, if we are to live fully functioning lives three key processes are needed:

1   The brain needs to discriminate between different sensations, focus on what's important and ignore the rest, i.e. 'habituate' to avoid wasting energy and overloading the body and mind with sensory information.
2   The sensory information needs to be understood; discriminated from other sights, tastes, touch and sounds; stored and accessed; and connected with meaning.
3   The different sources of sensory information need to be integrated to work together to provide us with an accurate representation of the world around us.

It is these connections that are fundamental to learning and memory. More sophisticated and with greater capacity than the most cutting-edge computer, much of the workings of the brain remain a mystery.

Sensory processing and perception

'The process by which an organism collects, interprets and comprehends information from the outside world by means of its senses is called perception' (Bogdashina 2003: 37). The term 'sensory processing' refers to how we use the information provided by our senses to make sense of the surrounding environment and to decide on possible courses of action. The process of sensory perception is characterized by four key stages, as shown in Table 2.3.

Table 2.3   Stages of sensory perception

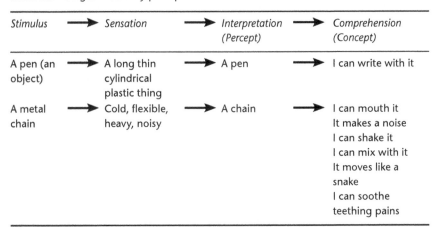

Stimulus	→	Sensation	→	Interpretation (Percept)	→	Comprehension (Concept)
A pen (an object)	→	A long thin cylindrical plastic thing	→	A pen	→	I can write with it
A metal chain	→	Cold, flexible, heavy, noisy	→	A chain	→	I can mouth it It makes a noise I can shake it I can mix with it It moves like a snake I can soothe teething pains

Source: Adapted from Bogdashina 2003: 37

The sensation stage does not analyse sensory information, but simply categorizes sensation into pleasure, pain, taste, touch, smell or heat. The interpretation stage takes place in the special areas of the brain responsible for processing that particular sensation. It is at the comprehension stage that a neuro-typically developed baby will learn to discriminate between useful sensations and therefore 'make sense' of the environment (Bogdashina 2003). Without some sort of system with which to classify and organize these sensory memories, an individual's ability to make sense of their environment would be time-consuming and severely limited. It is in this respect that the brain has developed sophisticated processes for categorizing and storing information, with easy retrieval the driving factor. Thus, in Bogdashina's example of a pen in Table 2.3, the final, comprehension stage involved linking the feeling of touching the pen with its function and the concept of writing. As we shall discover, this process of acquiring information and constantly checking its validity, in order to reshape understanding, forms the basis of infants' learning. Taking the case of a typical Treasure Basket session, an infant's encounter with a single object may be considered as an example of sensory perception. As can be seen from the chain example, just one Treasure Basket item can yield a host of sensations, concepts and associations – all of which will be carefully stored in a child's developing brain to improve future comprehension. Unlike prescriptive toys, the objects in a Treasure Basket have the potential to represent and be used for a multitude of things so the opportunities for developing richly connected neural networks increases.

Sensory perception is a prerequisite to the production of action or behaviour. Such actions need to emerge almost instantaneously and to constantly monitor, co-ordinate and reappraise changing inputs, all without us even being conscious of it! Eleanor Gibson (1969, cited in Bogdashina 2003: 40) suggests three mechanisms that help to achieve real-time responses, which I would summarize as follows:

1   The precision and consistency of children to discriminate stimuli improves with age.
2   The ability to attend to needed information and ignore irrelevant stimuli similarly improves.
3   By focusing on relationships and categorization, children are increasingly able to process several objects or events simultaneously.

Although all learning about the world ultimately stems from our senses, this is not a one-way process. Information from the sense organs or 'raw material' is influenced by the 'inside information' (or memories) that we have stored up about earlier experiences (Bogdashina 2003: 41). Similarly Pike and Edgar (2005: 75) point to the two-way nature of perception, describing it in terms of a flow of sensory information. To illustrate this in the context of a Treasure Basket, picture a group of children feeling objects in the basket. If they are trying to discover what an object is and what it is like, the flow of information from their tactile, visual and auditory exploration will be passing to their perceptual systems in the brain. If, however, the infants are trying to find a particular object in the basket, the information flow will be in the opposite direction. They will use their existing knowledge of what they are seeking to guide and make sense of the new sensory information. So for children looking for a metal chain, their eyes will be seeking out shiny objects, their ears attuned to the tinkling sounds of the chain and their tactile sense searching for something cold, bumpy, hard but flexible. Of course, for infants playing with the same Treasure Basket several times, the knowledge of discovered objects will be stored in their brain to call upon and reidentify the same objects or similar properties on other occasions. In essence 'you can think of sensations as food for the brain; they provide the knowledge needed to direct the body and mind' (Ayres 2005: 6). For young children, much of this knowledge is derived from the objects they encounter and so we now turn to the world of objects.

3 The world of objects

We know that babies' brains are growing fast, and that the brain develops
as it responds to streams of input coming from the baby's surroundings,
through the senses of touch, smell, taste, hearing, sight and bodily
movement. The Treasure Basket gathers together and provides a focus for a
rich variety of everyday objects chosen to offer stimulus to these different
senses. The use of the Treasure Basket is one way that we can ensure a
richness in the baby's experience when the brain is ready to receive, to make
connections and so to make use of this information.

(Goldschmied and Jackson, *People Under Three*)

Overview

To the untrained eye a Treasure Basket is simply a mismatched hotchpotch of
objects in a basket. But this same often 'misunderstood' resource can capture
and retain the interest of babies and children for significant periods of time.
Clearly there is more to this resource than meets the eye. In Chapter 2 we saw
how many foundations for learning are shaped through interactions with
objects thanks to the wondrous nature of children's developing senses and
brains. In this chapter we probe more deeply into the world of objects to shed
further light on the elusive appeal of a Treasure Basket.

Basket – criteria

As we shall discover in Chapter 4, the sort of basket that Elinor Goldschmied
would have been proud of would be round with straight sides, no handles,
sturdy enough to lean on, flat bottomed and smooth to touch. Crucially it

should be deep enough (10–12 centimetres) for its contents to be discovered bit by bit, rather than all in one go.

Basket – role

The basket provides an attractive and accessible storage solution, conducive to an enabling environment as children can access it themselves. However, its role may potentially be much more significant. The basket also helps distinguish this resource, making it all the more special and unusual. Its naturalness sets it apart from other toys. Picture the same Treasure Basket contents in a plastic or cardboard box, and a very different look, feel and appeal would be achieved. Not unlike a 'rummage box' that you might find at a charity sale, it would still be a magnet for children, but perhaps their expectations would be different, that of trying to find a bargain rather than of quality objects to be explored.

Over and above this it is suggested that the basket may actually serve to 'frame' the resources, much as a good picture frame and mount completes a picture and draws the eye to the artwork. In the same way that a different style and quality frame changes the look and 'feel' of a picture, so too a good quality basket sets off the contents of a Treasure Basket. It is also suggested that the 'containing' role of the basket may positively increase the appeal of the objects. One mother anecdotally described how her 8-month-old appeared to play differently with the objects when they were in the basket, rather than loose on a mat. Although the objects were apparently of equivalent interest, quality and distinctiveness, his play was much more focused and sustained than when the objects were offered without the basket.

Research into the play behaviour of monkeys may also contribute to our understanding of the significance or otherwise of the basket. Over four days, nine toys were scattered on a large rock normally frequented by the monkeys for play. These toys (and the rock) were actively avoided by the monkeys to the point that the researchers had to remove the toys for fear that the monkeys would change their behaviour. Toys that were spread out were not played with – only those that were 'bunched up' or being handled by another monkey. Finally 20 novel objects were left together under a crate in the woods. The next morning all the toys except two rubber snakes had disappeared and were found scattered around the tree canopy for some distance, having been played with by the monkeys. When repeated with fewer objects the same pattern emerged (Menzel in Bruner *et al.* 1976). How the objects were offered was found to be key in determining play, perhaps providing food for thought when it comes to a Treasure Basket?

The associative role of the basket is perhaps clearer. Given some infants' excitement simply at the sight of a Treasure Basket being placed before them, it is highly feasible that the basket has come to be associated with the experience of play and exploration. As such, the extent to which a basket is different to other toys helps make the resource, its contents and the opportunities it presents all the more special.

Treasure Basket objects – criteria

A Treasure Basket should contain 50 to 100 objects, all picked for their special qualities and sensory appeal. The natural and household objects should be scaled for child-sized hands and include a mix of shapes, colours, textures, properties and sizes.

Figure 3.1 A carefully crafted Treasure Basket

Objects – role

Garvey devotes a whole chapter to the unique characteristics of play with objects (Garvey 1986: 44–60). Objects also form an essential ingredient of the Learning Tools developed by Geoffrey Waldon, vital 'learning-how-to-learn tools, mental tools which all children use to learn about the world around them' (Stroh *et al.* 2008: 13). Although much of this work is now several decades old, it nonetheless offers a valuable and highly relevant addition to the debate – a Treasure Basket essentially being about play with objects. At the opposite end of the spectrum, emerging neurological findings can also advance our understanding of the significance of objects for children's play and learning, an area which has received relatively little attention. Collectively, perhaps, this can help unlock the key to understanding children's fascination for collections of objects, such as those found in a Treasure Basket.

The historical perspective

'Finding out what things are, how they work and what to do with them occupies a great deal of attention and effort of the toddler and young child' (Garvey 1986: 44) and has close parallels with Treasure Basket play. Garvey suggests that

> Objects serve as a link between the child and his environment in a number of ways. They provide a means by which a child can represent or express his feelings, concerns, or preoccupying interests. They also provide a channel for social interaction with adults or other children. Further, for the child an unfamiliar object tends to set up a chain of exploration, familiarization and eventual understanding: an often repeated sequence that will eventually lead to more mature conceptions of the properties (shape, texture, size) of the physical world.
>
> (Garvey 1986: 44)

To this list should also be added the role of objects as a tool for developing symbolic play. We will now look at each of these in turn.

Representing feelings, interests and concerns

Unless we watch children's play carefully, we risk missing the links between apparently discrete actions, failing to spot their prevailing interests or concerns. Like the 13-month-old baby with an obvious fascination with enclosure whose expression, when she discovered that a leather scrunchie fitted inside a saucepan-like object, appeared to convey a sense of achievement and surprise. I have seen similar 'eureka' moments: when a child balanced a rubber plug on the mouth of a tin and discovered it fitted perfectly; when an object was successfully fitted inside a cardboard box or metal tin and created a noise when shaken; when a snaking chain was tossed in a mini metal pan; or when the tiny coil of a tea ball chain was threaded through the looped end of a teaspout brush. There have been countless other examples. These moments reflect the culmination of deeply focused exploration, where children have clearly set themselves a challenge, be it tossing the chain in the pot or balancing an item on another, and they have achieved their goal. This type of play is typically indicative of 'high involvement' on the Leuven Involvement Scale for Young Children (Laevers *et al.* 1997), to which we will return in Chapters 5 and 6, and succinctly reveals the fascination of 'simple' objects.

Channel for social interaction

A key tenet of Broadhead's (2004) Social Play Continuum is the role of objects in sustaining play through the resolution of ownership issues. The giving and receiving of objects was found to make a 'key contribution to increasing or diminishing the levels of sociability and cooperation'. Broadhead notes the role of objects in the different stages of the Social Play Continuum as follows: In the 'Associative Domain', an object may be offered, as a possible indicator of reciprocity, but equally this may be ignored or an altercation may arise from an object being taken by a peer. In the 'Social Domain', offered objects are more likely to be accepted, and where a peer's object is taken without permission, compromise rather than altercation tends to arise. In the 'Highly Social Domain' the offering and accepting of objects is both a key aspect of building the social dimension of play and better integrated within the flow of play. A transition seems to occur in the 'Co-operative Domain', with objects being offered and accepted to develop and bring play themes and children's ideas to life. In this final stage 'the objects become incidental to relationship building and integral to problem-solving activities and goal achievement' (Broadhead, 2004: 46). Observations revealed children's protectiveness of objects and how 'objects were strongly associated with play continuity' (Broadhead 2004: 3), an issue to which we shall return in Chapter 7 when we explore the role of objects in supporting personal, social and emotional development.

Exploration, familiarization and understanding

Exploration is a cumulative process helping shape a child's concept of the world. Geraghty notes that

> concepts of colour, form, size and properties are developed as [a child] explores different materials . . . Discovery of the properties of different play materials leads [a child] to classify and categorise items to his own criteria.
>
> (1990: 194)

Making the links to Treasure Basket play and exploration, children can typically be seen exploring the objects with their hands and by mouthing them, as we found in Chapter 2. Returning to the sensorial image of a human being (Carter 1998: 117), with enlarged mouth and hands reflecting the areas of greatest sensory feedback, it is evident that the explorative processes typical of Treasure Basket play can support a child's development on several levels. Children can be seen developing key skills such as hand–eye co-ordination, tracking skills, fine motor skills – all vital for normal daily functioning. Less obviously, though, through mouthing and careful exploration with their hands, they will be discovering about the properties of objects, establishing a complex neural filing system for recording and categorizing a whole host of concepts key to understanding the world and developing 'thinking skills' (Klemmer *et al.* 2006, cited in Antle 2012). In fact Murray identified a range of approaches taken by children to the exploration of resources, from exploring objects *per se*; using them as props to facilitate other investigations; exploring properties as a precursor to using as props; and solving problems with resources, all of which have a close affinity with Treasure Basket resources (Murray 2011).

In one observation, a 19-month-old boy was seen apparently sorting, transporting and placing objects and then repeating this series of actions. The reasoning behind these actions is unclear but given his focus, motivation and perseverance, potentially 'high' or 'extremely high' involvement (Laevers *et al.* 1997), this suggests an underlying process of exploration, familiarization and understanding:

> He picked up the metal objects from the basket one by one and put them on a nearby table. He then returned them to the basket before repeating the same process several times.

Symbolic play

We referred in Chapter 1 to children's aptitude for divergent thinking and the relationship between this, a child's age and how realistic an object is. Bruner refers to the 'qualitatively different way' of playing brought about by symbolic play with objects (1974, cited in Garvey 1986: 45), a gradual progression which we will return to in Chapter 6. This 3-year-old boy's play captures the essence of using objects for symbolic play:

Child 3 (4 years and 9 months): 'I'm making ice cream.' Child L puts the 'pillow' in the tin with the 'nut' [tea infuser] on top and starts shaking. Child L uses the egg cups as eggs and the basket becomes the oven. 'Who wants some of my custard soup?' (shouts L). Child 2 (3 years and 2 months) is using the whisk. 'I'm making noodles.' Child 2 hands Child 3 a box in response for their request for flour. 'Thanks' says Child 3.

The importance of Learning Tools

Early play with objects lies at the core of the concept of Learning Tools developed by Geoffrey Waldon in the 1970s. Young children typically explore their environment 'meeting motor, perceptual and emotional needs' (Stroh *et al.* 2008: 13) and out of these explorations, patterns of behaviour begin to emerge. A series of cross-cultural Learning Tools are instinctively used by children to learn and solve problems. The eight tools of placing, piling, banging, pairing, matching, sorting, sequencing and brick building are closely interrelated, and identifiable in the play characteristic of early childhood and particularly Treasure Basket play.

The contribution of neuroscience to our understanding

As we discovered in Chapter 2, far from being 'empty vessels', babies' brains are amazingly sophisticated. Our understanding of the role of objects in young children's cognitive development has increased significantly in the last decade, thanks largely to a wealth of research, but a link between this and Treasure Basket play has not yet been made. Although none of this research focuses on Treasure Basket objects *per se*, it does offer useful insights into the unexplained appeal of this resource.

Recognizing and analysing objects

As described in Chapter 2, when visual information reaches the primary visual cortex, the information divides into two (or more) pathways before travelling to different parts of the brain. Although this is oversimplifying the process and understating the degree of interconnectivity, the dorsal stream is responsible for analysing information about the position and movement of objects, while the ventral stream is associated with pattern discrimination and object recognition. Put simply, the ventral stream is concerned with the question 'What is it?' while the dorsal stream focuses on 'Where is it?'

(Schneider 1967 and 1999, cited in Pike and Edgar 2005: 103). If an object is flying through the air at you, the priority is avoiding collision, rather than identifying the object, hence the need for different types of information to be provided at different speeds. As one might expect, the dorsal stream receives information faster than the ventral stream and offers only short-term storage. In contrast the ventral stream processes fine detail and is largely object-centred and knowledge-based, relying on information about recognized objects already stored within the brain. This distinction between the speeds of 'perception for action' and 'perception for recognition' originates perhaps in primitive 'fight or flight' responses.

When we watch a young child engaging with a Treasure Basket we tend to take for granted the magnitude of many of the actions played out before our eyes. Yes, we can recognize babies improving their fine motor skills, hand–eye co-ordination, pincer control and manipulative skills, but do we really appreciate the complexity of the 'behind the scenes' learning? Although the division of movement and object-centric information has been simplified, it does provide an insight into the degree of sophistication involved in analysing even simple objects, helping us to appreciate perhaps the significance and cognitive drain of what may wrongly be perceived as simple actions.

Object permanence

Piaget introduced the notion of 'object permanence', when a child realizes that an object still exists even when it cannot be seen, touched or heard, and this was found to be present at between 8 and 12 months of age. However, rapid advances in neuroscience have since revealed that children as young as 10 weeks 'recognise that an object continues to exist after it is hidden' (Baillargeon 1995, 1998, 2000, cited in Baillargeon 2002: 48).

Imitating and interpreting actions

Newborns imitate gesture actions such as mouth opening and tongue protrusion as early as 42 minutes after birth! This early matching behaviour indicates a close coupling between an infant's acts of seeing and doing. For infants to imitate an action they need to 'unify the seen acts of others and their own felt acts into one common framework' (Meltzoff and Moore 1983, cited in Meltzoff 2002: 11, 13). The degree of sophistication involved becomes clear when broken into its constituent parts – infants can only see the adult's actions, not feel them with their proprioceptive 'sixth sense', but they cannot see their own facial gestures and therefore can only monitor these by how they feel.

In Chapter 2 we considered the potential significance of a child's hand positions in terms of the type of information with which this might furnish the brain. We also discovered that newborns use their own experiences and actions to interpret the actions of others. According to Meltzoff and Moore (1983, cited in Meltzoff 2002: 22),

> Newborns bring [this knowledge of what it feels like to do the act] to their first interactions with people, and it provides an interpretive framework for understanding the meaning that lies behind the perceived movements.

This can be seen in action when a young child grasps objects from a Treasure Basket to explore. The experience of grasping to satisfy their urge to explore helps infants make sense of the goal-orientated grasping of others. When infants then see other people reaching for an object, they notice how they extend their hand and in particular the curled position of their fingers, inferring meaning to the action based on their own experiences. The development of imitative capacities and the sense that others are 'like me' is critical to making sense of the world. Conversely, for children where sensory processing difficulties exist, for example children with autism, they are likely to find it more difficult to understand others, as will be explored further in Chapter 8 (Meltzoff and Moore 1983, cited in Meltzoff 2002).

Analytical thinking

Another early rule in operation relates to what neuroscientists term 'support events', where infants are shown an image of a box on the edge of a platform and they judge whether the box would be stable if released. A variety of different shaped boxes (with different centres of gravity) and in different positions were shown to infants and 3-month-olds who concluded that any contact with the platform, i.e. with the box positioned on top or at the side, would remain stable. By just over a year, understanding has evolved such that infants now realize that an asymmetrical object will only be stable if the greatest proportion of the shape is supported (Baillargeon 2002: 53–4).This evolution of thinking offers great insight into children's potential thinking in relation to Treasure Basket objects. Between the ages of 6 and 12 months, infants will be refining their understanding of 'support' through exploring balance, proportional weight, shape and touch, all factors that they could explore through Treasure Basket play. Equipped with this knowledge, we can better interpret the potential thinking and learning behind what might appear to be simple or even accidental actions, and in doing so, imbue greater meaning to Treasure Basket play.

Quantitative and qualitative reasoning

Research has highlighted a distinction between children's use of quantitative (i.e. absolute facts such as height) and qualitative reasoning strategies that involve relative information, i.e. that object A is taller than object B. Five-month-old infants were found to be able to reason qualitatively about height information, rather than quantitatively, but further research is required to identify at what point a transition occurs (Baillargeon 2002). With this information in mind, it is entirely possible for young babies to be developing their qualitative reasoning while exploring Treasure Basket objects. As they sort through the objects in a basket, apparently without focus, this may in fact conceal comparative reasoning and rule development which will 'become richer and more complex with the identification of additional variables' (Baillargeon 2002: 57).

Specific rather than generalized learning

Research has demonstrated how infants 'sort' physical events into categories, and learn separately how each category operates (Baillargeon 2002) rather than generalizing information. Thus in experiments, infants of four and a half months treat the rules of containment (one object being put inside another) as distinct from the rules of occlusion (where the object is hidden by a barrier). It is not until infants reach the age of about twelve months that they can generalize information from different categories, e.g. the fact that they will be able to see the upper part of a tall object in a short container in the same way that they could if the container was simply a barrier instead. An infant observing a metal chain from a Treasure Basket being dropped in a tin, a spoon being placed in a cup or a crocheted mat being squeezed into a small box will not search for the commonality between the different experiences or events i.e. that the object in each example needs to be smaller than the container in order to fit inside, but instead will try to understand what is happening in each case.

By compartmentalizing events into different categories and learning separately about each category, it breaks down learning into smaller, more manageable chunks. This has very real implications for our understanding of children's play and exploration since, to an infant, objects placed side by side fall into a different category to the same objects stacked on top of each other. Similarly, Onishi (2000, cited in Baillargeon 2002) found that at 13 months, infants were able to judge correctly the stability of a tower of two boxes, but did not generalize this same reasoning to a stack of three boxes, as the latter has to be discovered and learnt. Again this has interesting ramifications for

Treasure Basket play as simply repositioning the same object in a basket alongside other objects might change the categorization and thinking about that object. Perhaps the problem-solving opportunities and affordance presented by Treasure Basket objects (explored more fully in Chapter 7) has its roots in the acquisition of general and specific rules. In the same way that infants appear to develop and revise rules about objects or actions based on their experiences, given enough experiences their thinking is able to evolve, enabling them to generalize information across different categories.

Experiential learning

Offering children sufficient experiences is vital if they are to encounter the unexpected outcomes which reshape and evolve their initially simplistic rules. Drawing upon the analogy of the parable of the blind men and the elephant (whereby six blind men encounter a different part of an elephant and are convinced that they can best describe the animal), if children only encounter an object or experience in a singular manner, their initial rule (or conclusion) will remain unchallenged, like the men variously concluding that an elephant is like a rope, tree, wall, and so on. It is only by offering numerous opportunities for challenging and refuting these conclusions that more sophisticated and accurate conclusions can be drawn. This leads Baillargeon to conclude that 'where no variation is experienced, no learning should occur' (Baillargeon 2002: 63). Put in this way, it is easy to see how offering open-ended objects can help infants create and reshape information categories and how the act of simply collating them within a basket may reframe, challenge and fine-tune understanding and cognitive reasoning. Take this mother's account of an 8-month-old playing with her Treasure Basket indoors, then in the garden:

> I observed her throw the objects and then watch to see if they rolled. Each time something rolled it seemed to encourage her to find something else that would roll. Her eyes stayed constantly on the object until it moved. After discovering that banging and throwing objects inside generated rolling, it was quite a different story in the garden. When we went outside with the basket, she started to repeat what she had been doing in the house. However, the garden wasn't providing the same results, because the grass was uneven and the objects were not rolling as much, so she became frustrated. Once she found an area for the objects to roll on outside she seemed happy again.

Infants increasingly accurately predict outcomes because they develop a series of 'condition–outcome rules' (Baillargeon 2002: 80) determined by their exposure to contrastive outcomes. These trigger a quest to understand what has happened and infants build causal explanations based on prior knowledge. Clearly, in both instances, play with Treasure Basket objects offers countless contrastive opportunities as well as the ability to create prior knowledge. This points to the importance of children being exposed to and physically enacting as many different variables as possible in order to extend their understanding of the general rules that govern the world. For example, Baillargeon (2002: 65) suggests that it is only when children are sitting independently at about 6 months of age that they are likely to encounter and understand 'support variable' experiences first-hand by actually placing objects themselves.

Categorizing information

In order for the brain to function effectively and rapidly retrieve information, a system of categorization is needed. These 'mental files' are akin to a state of the art filing system. As adults, we rarely encounter objects or events that we cannot easily categorize yet, for the infant, this is how the world is experienced. More commonly this occurs subconsciously, storing information alongside other similar or interrelated information and memories. Unlike the average one-dimensional office storage system, the same information, memories and images are linked in a multitude of ways to numerous other pieces of information, so that they can be quickly accessed in several ways. Thus the word 'forest' conjures up numerous words, memories, images, feelings and sounds.

Activity 12

Gather some unusual household or hobby-related objects that will not be universally familiar. Invite colleagues to try to guess what the objects are used for. Talk about how they might categorize the objects and what it must be like for a child, for whom anything and everything is label-less.

When we encounter something that we cannot easily categorize, we need to think carefully about the general meaning or concept that applies in order to store this knowledge. For an infant trying to make sense of the world, every object and encounter is new and needs to be 'understood', labelled and categorized. As we have already discovered, a necessary stepping stone in achieving this is for infants to break learning into small chunks and develop a series of rules about objects and events. Although not necessarily wholly accurate, these initial rules are constantly reshaped by new understanding, forming the basis of concepts as they give meaning to the attributes and behaviours expected for that category. For example, metal objects feel cold and make a noise when banged while fabric feels warm and soft. It is this aspect of categories which greatly assists memory as the words cat or ball, for example, come to denote a series of characteristics like 'has four legs and a tail' or 'rolls' and only information unique to that particular cat or ball, such as 'three-legged' cat and 'Fulham Football Club' ball need to be remembered. Freedman and Assad (2006, cited by Bornstein and Mash 2010: 884) conclude that categorization is 'a fundamental process by which the brain assigns meaning to sensory stimuli, and . . . is critical for rapidly and appropriately selecting behavioural responses'. Evidence for the existence of some type of categorization system in the brain is borne out by the experience of patients who have suffered brain damage and lose the ability to recognize certain objects but not others.

Bruner *et al.* suggested that 'to categorise is to render discriminably different things equivalent, to group objects and events and people around us into classes, and to respond to them in terms of their class membership rather than their uniqueness' (1956, cited in Braisby 2005: 164). As we have already discovered, for infants this requires a fundamental shift in thinking given that the early concepts and rules developed relate to individual objects and events rather than being generalized. In order therefore for a transition to occur to categorizing objects and events according to their similarity, a child first needs to have accumulated and revised rules about objects and events gained from a wealth of different experiences. A Treasure Basket provides a perfect testing bed for an infant to discover about the attributes and 'behaviours' of different objects; for ascribing and revising simplistic rules; and for developing concepts and categories. However, as we shall discover in Chapter 9, the adult's role in this process is crucial if the full potential of this resource is to be realized. This means providing an environment conducive to open-ended play. It's important to avoid influencing play or inadvertently introducing functional fixedness – the idea that by using an object in one way fixes its function, limiting creativity (Brown and Kane 1989, cited in Goswami 2002: 287). An example could be in using a Treasure Basket object in a particular way in the context of play.

Links to schema

We have seen the importance of children being exposed to 'contrastive outcomes' (Baillargeon 2002: 65) in order for them to develop their understanding and that some rule-based skills coincide with a child's opportunity to physically test his or her thinking. Might then this process of category formation be associated with their greater mobility and independence and the physical opportunities for testing and developing rules that this presents? When children are seen exploring schema (repeated patterns of behaviour), frequently this occurs in a full-bodied way as well as on a micro-scale, with them physically enveloping, transporting or rotating themselves (as we will discover further in Chapter 4). Given the importance of young children's learning being physical and its benefits to cognitive development, perhaps schemas represent children's physical enactment of rules and are a necessary precursor to developing categories of information.

Many practitioners will recall the 'lightbulb' moment of seeing a schema in action. Suddenly the link between many of a child's actions becomes apparent and their behaviour better understood.

> As a result of applying a range of action schemas to objects, infants arrive at the generalisations that objects are 'throwable', 'suckable' and 'bangable'. An infant may perform one schema on a range of objects, or a wide variety of schemas on one object.
>
> (Foss 1974, cited in Meade and Cubey 2008: 5)

We know that children's bodies and minds are biologically and socio-culturally driven to explore and satisfy these urges (Bruce 2005, cited in Meade and Cubey 2008) but have not explored the potential links between schema and the rule acquisition process, whereby children use their bodies to explore and refine concepts.

One observation in an Activity Centre revealed a number of potential schema. A 17-month-old boy explored enclosure and banging until a moment of discombobulation – two balls landing nearby sparked a flurry of trajectory exploration with several different balls. Another boy aged approximately 18 months appeared to display an enveloping schema as he methodically tidied all the objects into the basket (while other children were still playing), then lifted the edges of the mat up and folded these over the basket, to literally enclose it. He picked up the wrapped-up basket to move it elsewhere, his arms enveloping the basket as he did so, an act that he repeated twice as the basket was initially unwrapped by another child to play with it. Once the basket was successfully stowed away, he sat with a basket of Christmas decorations, looking at the objects. He picked up a small pretend Christmas parcel, approximately 4 cm square, which he deftly unwrapped, removing the ribbon and gift tag before prizing his finger under the glued corner of the brown paper to reveal a cube of polystyrene. This child appeared to show an absorption in an enveloping schema and determinedly used the objects to pursue this. Bornstein and Mash (2010: 887) suggest that infants' ability to categorize increases with their familiarity with the objects themselves. This would appear to fit well with children's full-bodied exploration of objects through schemas.

This chapter has sought to demonstrate the amazing sophistication and complexity of the brain, unpicking what may be misconstrued as simple actions, and revealing babies' mastery of difficult tasks. Historical and contemporary evidence has introduced a new way of understanding the underlying significance of Treasure Baskets in terms of play with objects, albeit wow-laden, sensory-rich objects. Throughout the book we will return to the workings of the brain in relation to the identification and analysis of objects, the fundamentals of most early learning. This should help illuminate some of the wonders of this special type of play, ensuring that proper weight and value are attached to Treasure Basket exploration. In the next chapter our focus turns to how Treasure Basket play manifests itself as a series of behaviours and activities.

4 Introducing Treasure Baskets and heuristic play

The Treasure Basket provides a whole world in focussed form because it is deliberately collected to embrace a part of what is there.

(Elinor Goldschmied, cited in Hughes, *Developing Play for the Under 3s*)

Overview

This chapter introduces the concept of Treasure Baskets, a pioneering and sensory-rich approach to play developed in the 1940s. The principles, characteristics and benefits of Treasure Baskets and their distinction from themed collections are explored, together with typical Treasure Basket behaviours. The chapter concludes by introducing heuristic play and loose parts play and suggesting the idea of a Sensory Play Continuum for extending the use of Treasure Baskets with older children.

The Treasure Basket

What is it?

As discovered in Chapter 1, the idea of a Treasure Basket dates back to the 1940s when Elinor Goldschmied observed babies' fascination for playing with collections of natural and household objects. Essentially a Treasure Basket is a sturdy natural basket brimming full of 'treasures' picked for their variety, sensory appeal and interest. The aim is to create a collection of beautiful objects, each selected for its own merits and 'wow factor'. Although at a glance a Treasure Basket may appear incredibly simple, in reality it 'is a very sophisticated concept' (Goldschmied, cited in Hughes 2010: 7). It should offer rich sensory appeal, open-ended play potential and, in my opinion, cross-cutting interest to children of different ages and interests. These attributes set it apart from conventional toys and also hint at the personal, social, emotional, physical, problem-solving and creative benefits to be gained.

Benefits

A carefully crafted Treasure Basket can support personal, social and emotional development generally, developing concentration, decision-making, independent and collaborative play. It gives meaning to language and develops fine and gross motor skills and hand–eye co-ordination. Problem solving and early number skills are brought to life. Understanding about properties and tool use naturally follow and creativity and imagination are inspired. As this shows, the benefits of Treasure Basket play are manifold, as will be explored in Chapter 7.

Creating a Treasure Basket with a 'wow factor'

If you've never seen a child playing with a Treasure Basket, hopefully the list of potential benefits will have sufficiently whetted your appetite to make you want to start your own collection! A Treasure Basket is quite simply a basket full of natural and household objects or 'treasures', so you will need the following.

The basket

Materials and size

Ideally the basket should be made from wicker or natural material with a diameter of 25–35 cm and a depth of 10–12 cm. Elinor Goldschmied provided quite prescriptive guidance on the specification of the basket (Goldschmied and Jackson 1994: 96–7). One consequence of this is that I have encountered parents and practitioners who have simply not offered this resource because they 'couldn't find the right basket'. As we explored in Chapter 2, the basket is clearly a vital element of this resource, serving to frame and present the resources attractively as well as providing storage. But I believe children are sufficiently enterprising to get the most from a basket that is not round, has small handles and differs from the dimensions specified by Goldschmied. In my opinion, it is far better for children to be offered the opportunity of playing with the resource than to deny them on the grounds of difficulties in sourcing a perfect basket.

Shape

A circular basket makes an attractive change to other resources and when placed between a child's legs there are no corners to poke in uncomfortably. It also works well when the same basket is played with by more than one baby or child at the same time, although this is not essential.

Sturdy and smooth weave

More important is the weave of the basket, which should ensure that there are no sharp pointy edges likely to scratch. The basket should be rigid and sturdy enough to take children's weight, should they choose to rest their elbow on it, as suggested by Goldschmied (although this is not something that I have personally encountered). Strong straight sides and a basket with some weight will help add to its rigidity.

Depth

If struggling to source the 'right basket', the next most important feature is its depth – it should be deep enough for children to have to dig through to find objects and experience a sense of discovering 'real treasure'. One practitioner was reflecting in a training session upon how the Treasure Basket in her setting was not used by the children and it became apparent that the basket had a large 'footprint' but was very shallow. Not only had they struggled to fill it with scaleable and attractive objects but, due to its shallowness, all of the objects were clearly visible, offering no incentive for children to delve in, so a key appeal of the resource was lost.

No handles

Goldschmied's exacting standards similarly rejected the idea of using a basket with handles. While clearly some large handles do have the potential to get in the way and disrupt hand movements and hand–eye co-ordination, the same is not necessarily true of small handles, or hand holds incorporated into the weave.

The Treasure Basket contents

Quantity of objects

The basket should contain 50 to 100 natural and household objects, picked for their sensory appeal, quality, play potential and impact. As the objects in

Figure 4.1 show, these should be child-size in scale and each contribute something to the overall sensory balance. Clearly the number of objects needs to be proportionate to the size of the basket, so bear this in mind when selecting a basket. That is not to suggest using an inappropriately small basket, but rather to emphasize the importance of the basket being full to the brim with beautiful objects, while still affordable.

Quality of objects

When creating a beautiful Treasure Basket the art is in persevering to ensure that the entire collection of objects has a 'wow factor'. To achieve this, items should be selected both for their individual and collective value and appeal. Elinor Goldschmied describes this perfectly:

> If you put a common object in the treasure basket it has to be a very good one, not inferior, otherwise the treasure basket becomes the rubbish basket, and that is why a badly collected treasure basket is the worst possible advertisement because it denigrates something which could be, should be appreciated – therefore it's got to be safe, it's got to be beautiful.
>
> (Goldschmied 1987 [DVD])

I have seen Treasure Baskets of interesting and sensory-rich objects ruined by the addition of over-sized and inappropriate objects such as an empty cardboard tissue box, a coat hanger and large pieces of bubble wrap or fabric, simply added to fill the basket. Far better to include fewer objects initially, all appropriately scaled and with their own intrinsic quality and appeal, than add inferior quality objects that undermine the appearance of the resource and mask the other treasures.

This is important on two key levels. First, children are drawn to and discerning about the beauty in resources and environments so it does matter what things look like. Secondly, if a Treasure Basket offers a whole spectrum of tantalizing glimpses of different coloured, shaped and textured objects, the natural instinct is to delve in and explore. Contrast this with a basket containing over-sized pieces of fabric or large objects and the difference and appeal are apparent. Not only do they conceal what lies below, but in my own view they dampen the desire to bother to look. Although a labour of love, creating an unusual collection of beautiful objects, gathered over time, will pay dividends in terms of the quality of children's play. Anyone who has ever created their own collection will probably understand the concept of 'Treasure Basket goggles' – the ability to spot rich pickings for a Treasure Basket in everyday life. This skill is certainly not the preserve of adults as my then 3-year-old, collecting items for her baby brother's basket, regularly

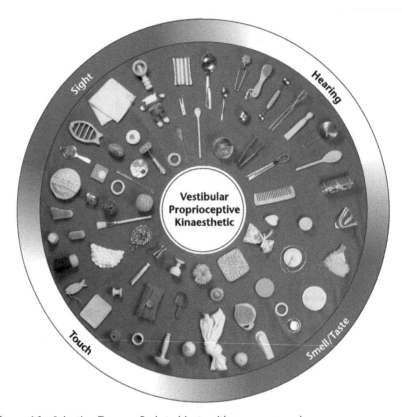

Figure 4.1 Selecting Treasure Basket objects with sensory appeal

demonstrated! Inspiring a love of collecting has also been cited by several parents as a welcome by-product of Treasure Basket play.

Sensory appeal of Treasure Basket objects

In Chapter 2 we explored each of the senses, focusing on how they operate individually and together to provide sensory information. Since sensory interest lies at the core of a Treasure Basket's appeal and is key to its benefits, it is essential for objects to be selected with this in mind. Table 4.1 provides some pointers for maximizing the sensory appeal of your Treasure Basket, as well as a useful checklist for ensuring that a collection offers all-round sensory appeal.

Like many adults reflecting upon play in their childhood (Papatheodorou 2010: 18), you may recall memories like Goldschmied's of climbing trees, making mud pies or rose petal perfume, playing with pots and pans or 'Granny's button box' and the endless play potential that these simple objects

Table 4.1 Maximizing the sensory appeal of Treasure Baskets

Sense	Sensory-rich ideas
Sight	Ensure objects are of varying colours, tones and patterns to provide visual interest. It is important to provide a balanced palate of naturally coloured objects as well as accent colours, to avoid visual overload and distinguish this resource from other brightly coloured toys. It is not necessary for colour to be restricted to black and white. Select items with a range of features and characteristics, e.g. plain, patterned, shiny, dull, big, small, clear, opaque, natural, etc. Provide a number of containers and objects that can be used for hiding things in; these may also support an infant's own experiments such as those in Chapter 6.
Sound	Offer objects with a range of different properties to maximize the potential for exploring noise-making. Metal will make a very different sound to wood and may not be regularly encountered by children. Containers that can be filled with other objects make great shakers. Alternatively containers that can be banged with hands and long-handled objects create wonderful drums and beaters. Some children enjoy simply blowing into a container, feeling the vibration, the heat of their breath and satisfaction of the sound.
Touch	Provide materials with different properties e.g. metal, wood, fabric, cardboard, rubber, stone, shell, wicker, pottery, thick glass, etc. This will provide a sensory *smorgasbord* of textures and properties like smooth and rough, warm and cold, heavy and light, soft and hard, prickly, etc.
Smell	Although few children consciously smell items in a basket this is not to say that this doesn't happen generally, through mouthing or play. With careful thought when selecting objects this, our most underused sense, can be appropriately stimulated. If you focus and take time you will discover that most objects such as rubber, leather, metal or wood have their own distinctive smell. Provide olfactory interest through the inclusion of metal, leather and rubber items (not plastic), a lavender bag, fresh orange, lemon or lime, pricked first with a fork, as a temporary addition (be sure to check regularly and remove before it goes mouldy). **Check allergies first.**
Taste	Many children will instinctively mouth the Treasure Basket items as this is a natural phase in exploration and, as we discovered in Chapter 2, provides infants with vital information. For this reason, items should be chosen that are safe to be mouthed, regularly checked and cleaned with soapy water and replaced when needed. Older children may be seen mouthing unfamiliar objects to try to understand what they are. This is a perfectly natural step in exploration, problem solving and discovery and is typically seen when a child encounters a 'wow' object, such as a whole dried orange, chamois leather scrunchie, or handmade item which they are trying to categorize and understand.

and environments offered. Young children have a well-observed fascination with the detail and play potential of everyday objects that can be difficult for adults to understand. It is important to have opportunities for self-driven exploration to remind ourselves of the wonder of simple objects.

Activity 13

- Sit comfortably with a pillowcase or bag of natural and household objects e.g. a plug, wooden spoon, teaspoon, whisk, etc. or an actual Treasure Basket. Take the time to feel the objects with your eyes closed as with the prominent visual sense removed it will free you up to experience other sensory domains.
- If you find an object that intrigues you, try to resist peeking. Simply put the object to one side so that you can look at it at the end.
- Once you've fully explored the collection, look at the objects and see which if any of them you find most appealing. Note whether these are the same objects that you enjoyed feeling.
- Try putting the collection in an attractive basket to see if and how this changes the appeal of the objects for you.
- Now compare with a selection of conventional toys, like those used in **Activity 3**. How do the two sets of objects compare? Which is more interesting and appealing, and why?
- Which set of resources did you prefer the feel of? Did the process trigger any memories?
- Repeat on your own without other adults or children present, and try outdoors instead.
- What did you most enjoy playing with, where and how?
- What, if anything, surprised you?
- What would you like to do differently or explore more of again another time?
- Did you find any difference between how you played and how you felt when playing with the different resources indoors/outside, alone/with others?
- Has this changed your view of Treasure Basket play?
- Is there anything you would change about what you offer children, e.g. time for play, contents of the basket, whether the basket is offered on a mat (to create a 'zone' and increase focus), space, frequency, time of day offered, length of time for which the resource is offered, where it is offered, accessibility of basket, age of children offered the resource, etc?
- Is there anything that you would change about your role, e.g. less hands-on, more supportive, more focused observations?

Key principles of Treasure Basket objects

Natural versus plastic

Both Goldschmied and Hughes emphatically suggest the avoidance of plastic in a Treasure Basket. I personally agree, as this makes the resource all the more special and unique, but many practitioners choose to include plastic items. If debating what to include I would urge practitioners to try non-plastic objects first to see how this impacts upon children's play. However, if choosing to add plastic items, these should pass the same 'tests' as the other objects, i.e. be special in their own right and offer a rich sensory contrast, rather than simply being included because they are easily sourced, cheap and child-sized.

Recent practitioner-led research explored what happened when two identical mats were laid on the floor in a room, one with conventional plastic toys on it, the other with Treasure Basket objects. Over a number of sessions the practitioners observed which resources the children chose to play with. The results were resounding, with all the children selecting the open-ended Treasure Basket objects in preference to the plastic toys. A Treasure Basket can be seen as the 'iPad' of the natural world and as we shall discover has particular value for its open-ended play potential, with any object capable of being used for, or becoming, whatever a child wishes.

Toys versus non-toys

The addition of real toys, like mini-characters, should similarly be avoided as this significantly erodes the open-ended qualities of a Treasure Basket. This is particularly true of branded or licensed toys, which introduce an age-appropriate dimension that does not otherwise exist. The inclusion of featureless 'figures', like a teddy or gingerbread person, that can be shaped by children's imagination can, however, contribute an interesting sensory and representational dimension to Treasure Basket play, as we shall discover in Chapter 6.

Novelty

Babies and young children's brains are hard-wired to search for novelty and pattern (Brierley 1994: 90), so a carefully sourced Treasure Basket can provide literally a 'world in a basket' as Goldschmied describes (1987). So strong is the appeal of novelty to babies that it actually forms the basis of most baby-based research (Starkey and Cooper 1980, cited in Bryant and Nuñes 2002: 414). It is important to include objects with a 'wow factor' as they greatly extend the appeal of this resource. Take these two children's experience:

S (aged 2 years and 10 months) picks up the whole dried orange and shakes it. A smile spreads across her face. She looks into it and tries with a few objects to pull the orange apart and get the inside out. S picks up the clay pebble-shaped item with coloured glazed indentation: 'Wow, it looks like soap.'

This same object in a pre-school aged child elicited a question to the practitioner: 'What is it?' The practitioner shrugged her shoulders and the child paused and then exclaimed, 'It's a jammy dodger!'

Several factors help contribute to the novelty and appeal of this resource, from their sensory-rich dimension which contrasts markedly with mainstream 'toys'; the inclusion of often 'forbidden objects', such as pottery, glass and metal, which command respect and awe; and the highly contrasting objects, textures, materials and properties which inspire creativity and problem solving. The unique qualities of each individual item help make this resource special, but their juxtaposition with objects that you would not expect to find next to each other further adds to this, promoting endless opportunities for problem solving and creativity. Even very young babies sit happily absorbed in play for an hour or more and for older children too they offer endless opportunities for play and problem solving.

The context

Although not a factor referred to by Goldschmied, the immediate environment in which the Treasure Basket is offered may also have a bearing upon how the resource is used. Anecdotally, numerous practitioners have referred to increased concentration, focus and improved learning outcomes when the basket is offered on a neutral floor mat. The potential importance of this first became apparent to me when observing sessions at a playgroup and primary school. In both instances the floor coverings were highly patterned, so when the objects were removed from the basket it was difficult to actually see them. A mat potentially fulfils a number of key roles:

- Providing comfort from the cosy material and a clean environment for play.
- Providing a visual focus, both in terms of attracting children in the first place and framing the resource once children are seated at the basket.
- Providing a virtual barrier to other play interruptions, as older children in settings tend to run around the mat.

- Providing a visual cue that play is about to begin, if the mat is used as part of a routine.
- Reducing visual overload for a child hypersensitive to visual stimulation.

Using a Treasure Basket

As we will discover in Chapter 9, the adult's role is essential in providing not just a well-maintained, stimulating resource but, crucially, the space and time for its unhurried exploration. Babies and children generally need no explanation or introduction to help them get the most from a Treasure Basket, rather it is we adults who may need to watch, listen and learn! Given 'permission' and the necessary space and time, children will contentedly explore for an hour or more at a time. An important starting point is clearing the room or outdoor space of other resources as this helps minimize other distractions. Ensure that the baby or child is sitting comfortably and safely on the floor, supported by cushions if needed. Position the basket next to or in front of the child, or group of children, and sit back and watch play. Avoid asking questions, offering particular objects or commenting on play; let the children show you what they are interested in, through their play. Some adults may struggle to take a 'back seat' and be prone to offer objects, comment, ask questions or even suggest play ideas, such as 'Try banging . . .' Not only can this interrupt children's train of thought but it can negatively influence play, restrict creativity and unhelpfully 'fix the function' of objects (we will return to the notion of functional fixedness throughout the book). Play with a Treasure Basket is one type of play where it is vital for children to be allowed to play and explore fully and freely without fear of being judged or misinterpreted for how they play. Goldschmied described 'the Treasure Basket [as] an attitude of mind; an attitude of observation' (Goldschmied, cited in Hughes 2010: 6) and this clearly presents a challenge to some adults.

Activity 14

It may help to take some time out to explore a sand tray or Treasure Basket yourself. Alternatively, cast your mind back to a moment when you have been happily engrossed in something. It could be a favourite TV programme, a great book or a game.

- How did you feel when you were interrupted and abruptly pulled out of your own world?
- Can you see parallels with how a child might feel?

Stages of play

Piaget, and later Hughes, identified an indicative guide to understanding the process of play with objects. Early play is characterized by exploration as children focus on 'What is this object?' and 'What is it like?' With a natural curiosity to explore the properties of objects and the satisfaction of discovery, this can occupy children for hours. As children get older, they tend to play in a more complex way, combining objects and other resources to ask 'What can I do with it?' Finally children typically progress to 'What can it become?', where simple objects can come to represent whatever imagination inspires. Not to be confused with the Continuum Stages briefly outlined in Chapter 1, an awareness of these stages of play helps illuminate children's lengthy explorations and play with a Treasure Basket. This is age-related (typically babies aged 5–10 months will be seen exploring 'What is this object like?', children aged 10–20 months 'What can I do with it?', and 20 months plus 'What can it become?') (Hughes 2010: 2). However, older children encountering a Treasure Basket for the first time will also be seen to pass through these stages, albeit at an accelerated rate.

'What is this object like?'

The following 40-minute observation of a 6-month-old playing reveals the depth of exploration possible with just one or two objects!

> She grabs hold of the natural woven coaster. She turns it around and puts it to her mouth to mouth it. This action is repeated, turning it around, holding it and putting it back in her mouth. This continues for at least 10 minutes before she picks up another object, the tea strainer, and puts it in her mouth. She mouths it for at least another 10 minutes before taking it out and holding it. She picks up the coaster and alternates between mouthing this and the tea strainer for 40 minutes.

'What can I do with it?'

As this observation shows, the concepts of 'What can I do with it?' and cause and effect are very closely related, particularly when offered with other resources in Stage 2 of the Sensory Play Continuum.

> Boy aged 3 years picks up the tea strainer and takes it to the sand tray. He scoops up the sand and holds it over a metal spatula to sprinkle. He pauses as the sand and rice mixture doesn't come

through the holes . . . He picks up the metal spoon and holds the large swirly shaped shell steady while he pours the sand into the 'mouth' of the shell. He picks up the large metal spoon and holds the handle end so that just the tip of the spoon strikes the pumice. After each blow he pauses and examines the stone intently with his eyes while feeling with his fingers [as if expecting it to be chipped or dented by the metal, perhaps?].

'What can it *become?*'

As well as engaging in domestic role-play or super hero play, children transform objects in a multitude of ways, like this observation in a family home where a visiting 9-year-old plays with the Treasure Basket:

> . . . She began to try and make things by putting them together and then appeared to change her mind. She made one big body on the floor using numerous objects. The peg became the nose, the cloth became the hair, the chamois leather scrunchie became the mouth, the pebble and the plant pot were eyes, the tin was the neck, the plug was the heart 'With a vein coming out' she said [pointing to the chain of the plug]. She continued with the rest of the body giving a reason for all of her choices, like the eyes, 'The pebble has a smaller circle inside for the pupil and so does the plant pot. That's why they make perfect eyes!'

We will return to this transition between exploration and imaginative play in Chapter 6. Suffice it to say that this is not the only way that children's play changes with age. Garvey suggests that play also evolves from simple, one-item play to complex play with several items, as the above snapshots of play perfectly illustrate. There also seems to be a broad correlation between the advent of complex play with multiple objects and the transition from exploration to imaginative play.

Typical Treasure Basket behaviours

Although Treasure Baskets have been played with for the past 60 or more years, the type of behaviour and actions typically seen during play has largely eluded analysis or classification. To date attention has focused on describing play in terms of 'What is this object like?', 'What can I do with it?' and 'What can it become?' Although this is immensely helpful in understanding and describing play as it evolves, a focus on specific behaviours may add value to our interpretation of play, and in doing so perhaps stop us being so quick to intervene, interrupt or take over children's play. It was with this in mind that a series of typical Treasure Basket play behaviours have been developed as an observational tool to try to unlock the particular appeal of object play for children across the ages. Using the Learning Tools (introduced in Chapter 1) and a number of video observations as a starting point, 31 frequently observed Treasure Basket 'behaviours' were identified (*Exploratory play* 2006; Papatheodorou 2010). As an observational tool it was important for this to be readily useable by parents, so the activities were limited to one side of A4 paper. Although artificially constrained by the page size, this was felt to offer a good starting point for carrying out observations. Following use, the table was further modified by the introduction of categories of types of activities, such as movement, pretend play, etc., to assist quick identification.

The observation sheet (see Appendix 1) was used for the majority of the sessions, without any reported user difficulty. Although there is clearly scope for debate about where best to slot particular activities – for example, mouthing is essentially a placing activity as well as exploratory – it does provide a useful starting point in exploring Treasure Basket play behaviours more fully. The classification introduced within Appendix 1 is not intended as a developmental box-ticking process, but rather as a vehicle for better understanding typical play behaviours; diagnosing obvious problems – where none of these behaviours are present; identifying different activities and emphasis in older children's play; and highlighting play commonalities. The framework was introduced in 20 sessions, with children of different ages and Continuum Stages, and provides a useful starting point in considering the following key Treasure Basket behaviours (distinguished in bold).

Movement-related behaviour

The following observation of a 17-month-old boy reveals a range of movements, repeated throughout the session with different objects. This may reveal an interest in cause and effect or perhaps a trajectory schema as the same child was also seen throwing lots of objects.

> He picks up a miniature metal bucket and a tea strainer, one in each hand, and jabs the pointed lip of the strainer into the bucket. It makes a noise. He repeats the action several times. He picks up the bucket and tea strainer and walks near his seated mother . . . He then tips up the bucket and makes a wafting scooping motion with the strainer . . . He holds the handle of the bucket then rests it against his leg and repeats the jabbing motion, but this time two-handed.

This child **picks up, places, throws** (in an earlier part of the observation), **uses both hands, waves** and **transports** the objects. The jabbing motion was separately recorded as this is less commonplace.

Figure 4.2 Treasure Basket play involves full-bodied exploration

Explorative behaviour

Explorative behaviours perhaps most explicitly demonstrate the 'sense-led' attributes of play. We saw in Chapter 2 how much information infants derive from the sense of touch, from sensory receptors in their hands or mouth. This child, aged 2 years and 4 months, who typically never mouths objects, does so repeatedly during play with the Treasure Basket.

> Child 5 has the plug and chain, mouthing the rubber of the plug all the way round. Child 5 picks up the clay stone, rubbing the green surface with her finger, then places the stone in her mouth, scratching the surface with her teeth.
>
> (Papatheodorou 2010:31)

During play with a Treasure Basket a small minority of children actively **use their feet** in play or exploration. Other infants wiggle their toes or wave their feet, seemingly with excitement, as the Basket is lowered before them. Take these examples of Treasure Basket play:

H, aged 7 months, babbles as he picks up the cylindrical tin with lid. He holds it with one hand and manoeuvres the top. He then uses his **feet** and two hands to turn the tin on end. The tin falls and his moving toes 'catch' the falling tin.

G, aged 13 months, spots the rubber plug on a chain at the top of the basket and takes it out. She then sits putting the chain through her toes and lifts her toes up using the plug. She plays with the chain, wrapping it through her toes, and then uses the plug to pull the chain through. She continues playing in this way for some time. She walks around the room carrying the chain and plug at all times. She then stops and looks at her uncle's toes. She pulls his flip-flop off and then experiments with his toes and the chain, in the same way that she had with her own. Her uncle says, 'Do you like my toes?' but she remains uninterrupted. She looks puzzled. He repeats the word 'toes' a few times and she looks up at him and smiles. She moves position in the room and again puts the chain through her toes.

Later that day, when asked 'Where are your toes?', for the first time she looks down at her toes. This session is noteworthy as she does not typically play with her toes.

In another session a baby girl repeatedly stretched out her leg, while holding her toes, and rested her foot on the basket edge, like a ballerina doing stretches. This behaviour had not previously been observed by the carer and happened apparently in an 'absent-minded' way while her play continued with the Basket.

Smell does not feature significantly as a discrete behaviour in most children's play with the Treasure Basket, other than while mouthing objects. For the following two children the wow factor of the whole dried fruit, with scored pattern detailing, may have attracted them to the object in the first place. 'Lime, smell this' says E, giving the lime to his carer. In a separate observation Child 5, aged 2 years and 4 months, picks up the orange, saying, 'Look, it smells like orange, that smell nice.'

Manipulation

As will become apparent in Chapters 5 and 6, numerous examples of manipulation are evident as children explore what objects are like and what they can do with them. Several babies and children have been observed manipulating objects, such as the rubber plug, carefully turning it with their fingers to enable them to mouth its edges. In fact it is questioned whether the explorative hand procedures identified by Lederman and Klatzky (referred to in Chapter 2) are manifest as hand movements and mouthing in infants. Although frequently manipulation is linked to mouthing, this is not always the case, with some children moving objects perhaps to understand them better or to discover what else they can do.

> He manipulates the strainer in his hand, turning it to hold it by the other end. He holds the handle of the bucket [which is folded flat against the bucket and quite stiff] and tries to manoeuvre it to form a handle.

Sound-making activities

Deliberate and accidental **sound making** are common features of play with Treasure Baskets in children (and adults) from across the ages.

> Boy picks up the metal bucket and turns it upside down. He puts it on the floor upturned, and bangs it with the 'head' of a wooden spoon. He continues banging before searching through the basket.

> Child 4 (2 years and 2 months) is shaking the tin, standing up. Child 4 carries on shaking the tin, but dances along with it (Sensory Play Research).

> J (2 years and 9 months) picks up the chain and pushes it in and out of the tin, listening to the noise, 'Oh'.

Whether this is a reflection of their fascination or satisfaction in exploring cause and effect; the enjoyment of the sound; the novelty of playing with non-plastic objects that make different sounds; because they feel this is what is expected given that so many observations involved adults themselves exploring and suggesting noise making, or some entirely different reason, it is impossible to say. Sound making generally appears to take three forms: banging things together, blowing into something, or rattling and shaking an object inside another. Take this example of blowing:

> The boy (aged 2 years and 6 months) walks around the room holding the cylindrical tin with no lid. He holds the tin up to his mouth and blows into it, making a noise. He picks up the wire eggcup and repeats the same action, making a noise into this instead. He takes the tin to his mum seated near the Treasure Basket and gives her the tin to speak into.

Some play sessions involve exploring sounds in several ways, for example banging a tin then rattling it with another object inside:

> He stands up and shakes the tin. It rattles as he shakes it from side to side.

Communication

The spoken word is just a tiny proportion of everyday communication, with body language both more prevalent and discernible at a younger age. For some children an expression on their face is a sure-fire indicator of pleasure or excitement and proof positive of the fascination of simple objects.

> A 16-month-old boy is sitting exploring the Treasure Basket with his father behind him. His eyes light up as he sees the pastry brush.

Although primarily a 'non-social' activity, watching babies and young children playing can have the appearance of a conversation:

> A 12-month and 9-month-old baby are sitting playing together with the Treasure Basket. As they play they both babble, interacting with each other and the basket. They explore and babble.

Babbling, language and communication, either verbal or body language, between children and their carers, are commonplace. As will become apparent from the numerous observations detailed throughout the book, babies and children look to carers for reassurance and to share a revelation; look at peers to discover what they are doing or playing with; and use pre-verbal language to express surprise, excitement, frustration or dissatisfaction or to share and communicate ideas. In some sessions unusual language responses were seen, as we shall discover in Chapter 6.

Problem-solving activities

It is a rare session that does not reveal problem-solving behaviour of some sort, with children typically seen putting objects inside one another, exploring mathematical concepts or exploring the properties of different objects through repeated actions, as this three-and-a-half-year-old appears to be doing.

> He hits the top of the metal pan with his hand. He hits the side of the basket with his hand. He breathes into the pan and then smiles. He hits the chain of the plug then uses the large rubber plug end to cover the pan ... He picks up the heavy metal choke chain, holding it up in the air so its other end touches the ground. It gently sways, making a tinkling noise. He holds both ends of the chain and loops them around each hand. He flaps the chain and it makes a 'crack' sound. It sways in the air. He holds up his arm outstretched

then holds the loop on the end of the chain, turning it with both hands. He looks at it, surprised. [Perhaps he expected the chain to roll up?]

In Stage 2 of the Continuum, when children combine resources, problem-solving behaviours are even more apparent, as we shall see in Chapters 6 and 7.

Pretend play

When children reach the 'What can this become?' stage, they will be seen engaging in pretend play with a Treasure Basket. Typically this will begin with domestic role-play, but in older children this develops into the more sophisticated world of fantasy or socio-dramatic play (Lowe, cited in Garvey 1986: 46).

> Child 4 (2 years and 2 months) undresses the baby with carer's help, picks up the loofah and cleans the baby: 'My cleaning my baby.' Child 5 (2 years and 4 months) says, 'I need a blanket for my baby.' 'Have a look in the basket.' Child 5 uses the dishcloth to cover the baby and helps the baby to go to sleep tapping its back. (Papatheodorou 2010)

It is all the more remarkable that a 17-month-old can engage in pretend play 'when they are just beginning to understand reality' (Lillard 2002: 205). Young children's ability to venture into the world of imaginative play is determined by a combination of their age and how representative or familiar an object is. For this two-and-a-half-year-old the two halves of a metal tea ball were sufficient prompt to be transformed into a speaking character:

> She walks over to me saying, 'Hello there' as she moves the lid of the tea ball with her fingers.

Similarly this 3-year-old created two characters in battle from the hooped ends of a metal chain:

> He lies on his back on the floor holding both ends of the chain in his hands above him. He makes talking noises as he moves the ends of the chain. He moves his thumbs.

Who is play suitable for?

Although originally intended for babies, play with a Treasure Basket offers older children something valuable and special too, through countless age-appropriate opportunities for problem solving, creativity, exploration and pretence. This is particularly true when offered as part of the Sensory Play Continuum (which we will return to in Chapters 5 and 6) as a mechanism for engaging older children in Treasure Basket play. The balance of control between adult and child shifts and the focus of play evolves throughout the cyclical stages (Gascoyne 2011). Children aged between 6 months and 6 years are likely to get the most from this type of play but this is not to deny their potential value to even younger children as some of the soft fabric items have been given to premature babies to provide much needed sensory stimulation. Obviously it is important to select the objects with care and to supervise at all times.

Watching children absorbed in play with a Treasure Basket is a magical experience and gives a fantastic insight not just into children's interests, developmental levels and schemas, but also their world. At the opposite end of the spectrum, adults with learning difficulties and even the elderly are enjoying the special appeal of play with a Treasure Basket, using them for exploration, manipulation, role-play, to inspire discussion or provoke memories. There really are no limits to play, as Goldschmied said: 'Everything is there and the only limitation is me' (Hughes 2010: 6).

The role of themed collections

Most early years settings will offer children a collection of objects of sorts, be it a container of brushes, metal objects, items found in a particular room, shiny objects, opposites, seasonal collections, and so on. Although of great value and benefit in their own way, none of these constitutes an actual Treasure Basket, although many may be described as such. A Treasure Basket is a collection of sensory-rich objects selected for their variety and differentness, whereas a key feature of themed collections is what the items have in common. Any number of different themed collections is possible (see Roberts and Featherstone 2002 and Hughes 2010 for more ideas). If considering a themed collection, first offer a Treasure Basket for play. Observe closely to discover what objects the child plays with and how. Equipped with this knowledge you can decide what collection to gather and how best to use it. It is helpful to distinguish between the different ways of using themed collections, be it for supporting a particular schema or interest; exploring characteristics, like rough, smooth, and so on; or extending a theme such as Christmas or the seasons.

Supporting schema or specific interests

If your observations reveal a child's particular interest in a type of object, or exploring a repeated pattern of behaviour, you can develop a collection of resources to support that child's particular needs. When a child with SEN displayed a strong preference for playing with the metal objects in a Treasure Basket a collection of metal objects was created to support this interest. Another child's play with a Treasure Basket revealed an enveloping schema as he repeatedly put objects inside each other or wrapped the objects up. For such a child a collection of containers, objects of different sizes and materials for wrapping these up may appeal. Many children display a transporting schema at some point in their development and so will enjoy being able to put small objects (or sand, water, dried rice etc. as suggested in Stage 2 of the Sensory Play Continuum) into a range of different containers. For a child with a transporting schema a collection of boxes, tins, bags, spoons for transporting and small items offer huge play potential.

Extending themes

A themed collection on the seasons, Christmas or different rooms of the house could be used to support a related book; develop a topic of interest; or, for children with SEN, to fuel their special interest. By adding an important three-dimensional and sensory element, this can help bring a story or discussion to life, sparking exploration and creativity.

Exploring characteristics

For collections based on characteristics, i.e. shiny, opposites, enclosure, big and small, and so on, first offer a traditional Treasure Basket for play, as that way children will be offered the full scope of choice over what to play with and how. Use these observations as a basis for planning a specific collection, if needed. Don't be tempted to rush this stage or to presume that a themed collection is the ultimate goal – this would be to underestimate the potential and appeal of Treasure Baskets.

Comparing a Treasure Basket and themed collections

The fundamental difference between a Treasure Basket and a collection of related objects is the theme or commonality, which will blatantly or subliminally influence play. So while a well-conceived Treasure Basket can be used to support special interests, schemas and topics of discussion, a collection of themed objects does not offer the same open-ended potential. Themed collections have a clear role and place within the early years environment, but should be seen as an alternative to the holistic experience offered by a Treasure Basket, not a substitute. Sometimes it is possible to label a child with a particular behaviour when the 'problem' may in fact be the resource.

The following observation provides a cautionary reminder of the potential limitations of themed collections.

> A 17-month-old boy comes and sits next to a basket of themed Christmas resources. One at a time he picks up an object, holds it for a matter of seconds before throwing it to his side or behind him with an impressive sideways movement of his arm. This continues until he's emptied the basket of its contents. He then moves to the 'real' Treasure Basket, using just four of the items in the basket (a metal bucket, tea strainer, large metal spoon and teaspoon), manipulating and exploring them and repeatedly making jabbing movements with these. He does not appear to be motivated by the effects of throwing, as he shows no interest in where the objects land. His play with the Treasure Basket reveals a very different, focused type of play.

The particular appeal of metal

Each child's experiences and preference will be uniquely different, but metal objects do seem to appeal on many levels as well as providing numerous opportunities for exploring cause and effect (holding a spoon and it warming up; filling a tin and creating a sound when shaken; banging two objects together and creating a sound) and trial and error. The appeal of metal should not, however, be taken as a signal to offer an all-metal Treasure Basket. As we shall discover in Chapters 5 and 6, much of the appeal of a Treasure Basket lies in the range of textures and properties on offer and children's ability to exercise choice over what and how to play.

Activity 15

In training sessions I use an enticing tray of sweets, biscuits, fruit (or even cheese) to explore the special qualities of a Treasure Basket. If you're considering introducing a themed collection of sorts, try this activity with colleagues or peers.

- Pick an attractive tray, platter or bowl. Gather a good selection of **wrapped** sweets (or one of the other options suggested). This should include sweets of different shapes, colours (shiny and opaque), sizes and flavours. Include some retro ones, like lemon sherbet or fruit salad, as well as recent inventions like Starburst. You are aiming for an enticing selection, some of which you will know from their wrapper and others that you will not.
- Pass the 'tray' around so that people can pick freely, then invite people to share which sweet (or biscuit, etc.) they picked and why.

Invariably the colour and shininess of a wrapper (or, if cheese or fruit, the unusualness, shape or colour) will have appealed to someone; the fact that they knew they were getting a mint or a toffee to others; and the chance to retrace memories sparked by a childhood sweetie, still others. Ask them to picture a room full of people they don't know and to guess which of the sweets (etc.) they might pick. Reflect upon the similarities between this and a Treasure Basket.

- Now ask them to reflect upon how they would feel if offered a tray of mints instead if they don't like or feel like eating mints? Which of the two trays would they prefer? Which would give them more scope for them to change their mind?
- Make the links to a Treasure Basket and themed collection and talk about how we can't assume that children will like what we do and how difficult it is to accurately second-guess which object a child might pick. It is only by offering a good assortment that adults (and children) can discover their likes and dislikes.

So far this chapter has focused on the Treasure Basket, developed by Goldschmied for babies, but transferable to older children too. Although the Treasure Basket remains the main focus throughout this book it is helpful to reintroduce two other forms of object play, as these provide both a context for the Treasure Basket and a possible direction for older children's play.

Heuristic play

Heuristic play, meaning literally 'discovery play', was the term coined by Elinor Goldschmied (in conjunction with Anita Hughes and Glen Carmichael) for play by 1- to 2-year-olds with lots of different objects. Heuristic play was seen as part of a natural progression from seated babies playing with a Treasure Basket, to mobile toddlers who thrived on this exciting new form of play. Heuristic play involves collecting lots of bags (twenty or more) each containing a similar type of object. So you might have one for curtain hoops, another for jam-jar lids and others for corks, balls, and so on. Although heuristic play itself was described by Goldschmied 'as a process not a prescription' (Goldschmied and Jackson 1994: 120), the adult's role, preparation and facilitation are in fact carefully set out, although the ensuing play is not. Once the collection is complete the adult's role is to clear the room of other toys and attractively arrange the mini-collections of resources on the floor. Several large tins, other containers and even a mug tree and kitchen towel stands are added for children to use for sorting. Children play uninterrupted, exploring the almost limitless permutations for play. This type of play is considered perfect for this age as children can incorporate their newly developed mobility and the proliferation of similar resources means they are not expected to share! Throughout play the adult subtly rearranges the collections – to help give 'clarity' to the resources; observes children's play; and allows sufficient time for unhurried tidying away. The adult orchestrates the process of sorting the different objects into their separate bags, with the children gathering these and the adult checking their condition, before storing safely away.

Activity 16

- Either select two or three existing bags of heuristic play items or gather together some objects to start a collection. Try hoops, e.g. napkin and curtain rings; jar lids; and balls, e.g. table tennis and golf balls, etc.
- Spend some time exploring the objects quietly. Experiment with using the objects in different ways. How many different ways can you come up with for using the objects?
- Play in a group instead and compare findings. Talk about what else you need to extend your play, e.g. large tins for collecting and sorting, a mug tree, a kitchen towel holder, different types of objects in other bags?
- Observe a session with children playing. What sorts of benefits, schemas (repeated patterns of behaviour like transporting, enveloping, lining up), examples of experimentation, trial and error, problem solving, sorting, etc. can you spot?
- Compare children's play and concentration with heuristic play and other resources.
- Has your play with the resources changed your feelings about this type of play?
- Reflect as a team on how best you can improve heuristic play provision for children, e.g. offer more frequently, change or add to the resources, reconsider the area in which they are offered, allow more time, and so on.

Loose parts play

Loose parts are large-scale environments, such as a beach, or materials such as tyres, crates, pallets and tubing that can be moved, combined, redesigned, lined up, taken apart and put back together in any number of ways within the confines of the environment (Brown 2009). Although the term was coined in the 1970s by Simon Nicholson, evidence of this type of play can be seen long before this in the resourceful type of play associated with postwar Britain (Anderson *et al.* 1962).

Like heuristic play and Treasure Basket objects, they have no specific set of instructions for being played with and can be used alone or combined with other materials as the individual wishes. As with their smaller counterparts, none of these resources would typically be described as toys. Their aim is to stimulate, facilitate and enhance children's play much like Treasure Baskets and to a lesser extent heuristic play (from an imagination perspective). Loose parts play involves full-bodied experiences and is great for problem solving, encouraging co-operative working, firing imagination and creativity, increasing physical development and supporting personal, social and emotional development. Depending upon the objects selected, they can be suitable from the age of one year up to and including secondary age children and can be enjoyed individually and collectively. As with Treasure Basket play the role of the adult is simply to provide a variety of interesting and safe resources in a safe environment, for children to access freely and play with. Watching loose parts play in action reveals astounding levels of creativity, problem solving and imagination.

Unlike Treasure Baskets, whose primary focus is sensory exploration (and the problem solving and creativity that this sparks), heuristic play offers collections of similar objects, selected more for their easy access and limitless play potential than sensory appeal. The resulting play may actually look very similar, with older children exploring cause and effect, trial and error, construction, sorting, patterns and problem solving as well as pretend play. When older children play with a Treasure Basket, many aspects of their play and experimentation could be described as heuristic play. The key factor in common is their affordance and the fact that there are no right or wrong ways of playing. This is true of both the treasures in a Treasure Basket and the objects in a heuristic play collection. Similarly, loose parts play is characterized by open-ended play with different objects and materials (some of which are sensory-rich), albeit on a much larger scale. So the plug or wooden spoon of a Treasure Basket, or curtain rings, corks and tins of heuristic play are replaced by car tyres, crates or sand of loose parts play.

Activity 17

Watch a loose parts play session then gather a selection of recycled resources, e.g. plastic baker's trays, car tyres, fabric, cardboard tubing, guttering, carpet offcuts and pallets, outdoors for you to experiment with other adults or children.

- Play freely, experimenting with the scrap resources.
- Complete a challenge, such as creating the most realistic mode of transport or coming up with the most uses and ideas for the materials.
- Solve a problem, e.g. getting to the other side of the playground without touching the floor.

Reflection

- Were there any discoveries, surprises, likes or dislikes?
- What implications, if any, does this have for existing provision?
- How did free play compare to being set a task or challenge?

As this chapter has shown, much of the quintessential appeal of a Treasure Basket derives from its quality yet open-ended objects. Like the items commonly found in a heuristic play set, natural treasures like twigs and seedpods or the large-scale crates, pallets and tyres associated with loose parts play, they have no right or wrong way of being played with, which makes them engaging, exciting, flexible and inclusive. We will now turn our attention to the three stages of the Sensory Play Continuum as a tool for extending Treasure Basket play.

5 Introducing the Sensory Play Continuum

This is a quest for understanding, and there is adventure in the satisfying of curiosity.

(Anderson *et al.*, *Activity Methods for Children Under Eight*)

Overview

This chapter introduces the Sensory Play Continuum (Gascoyne 2009) – a tool for extending the use of Treasure Baskets with children across the ages. Used as a framework rather than something to follow slavishly, the play potential of Treasure Baskets can be further expanded, and children supported to get the most from these stimulating resources. It also helps provide adults with a steer on when and how best to support play. Based on play observations with a Treasure Basket, we will discover how the three stages of play can assist us in getting the right balance between adult- and child-initiated play, as recommended in the EPPE report (Sylva *et al.* 2004: 37).

The Sensory Play Continuum was developed in 2009, inspired by numerous play sessions with children across the ages, not just babies. Based on observations of how children typically combine resources, it offers a tool for better understanding children's play with a Treasure Basket and for ensuring a good range of provision. At the heart of the Continuum is the balance between adult-initiated and child-led play which evolves through the following three stages.

Stage 1 – Free play

In this first stage, babies and children play freely with a Treasure Basket without any adult involvement. The emphasis for the adult is enabling free play without interruption, as suggested by Goldschmied. As such the adult's role is largely behind the scenes, providing a stimulating and safe basket of objects, ample space and time for free play, and observing play to inform future planning and provision.

What to do

Play

First check that the objects in the basket are safe to use and in perfect condition. Offer the basket, ideally on the floor, providing cushions for babies if needed. Sit nearby and watch children's play, resisting the urge to intervene. From time to time add new items to keep the resource fresh and exciting. A typical session may include play similar to this observation of a 9-month-old:

> She picks up the metal teaspoon in one hand and waves her arms with a positive expression on her face. She puts the teaspoon to her mouth and mouths it, making a loud 'Aaacchhh!' noise as she does so. She picks up the metal bowl while her other hand, still in a grasping position, touches the edge of the basket. She pauses, then her fingertips touch the wicker ball and uncurl to stroke and feel it again. She tries to pick up the wicker ball, moving her fingers to do so, but she can't lift the ball which is wedged in by another object. She picks up the teaspoon and holds it with both hands. She makes a loud 'Aaacchhh!' sound again. She turns the spoon to put the handle end in her mouth instead. She puts it in her mouth several times. She waves it and bangs it on the edge of the basket then drops the spoon. She picks up the metal tin and puts the (solid) bottom of it to her mouth. She looks surprised and looks at it. [So far her exploration has only revealed the open end.] She turns it, while holding the curved sides with fingers of both hands outstretched to grip the sides of the tin. She feels the bottom edge of the tin with her fingers before putting it down and picking it up again. She smiles as she manipulates the tin, enabling her to mouth a different part of the rim. It drops and she watches it roll. She picks it up with both hands.

The baby continues playing but the observation ceases as her mother explains to me how she doesn't normally play for such a long period of time or with this degree of absorption as normally she needs to be picked up. She is eager to know how to make her own Treasure Basket! Throughout the session the baby displayed good fine motor skills and hand–eye co-ordination. Her hand movements and manipulation of the resources revealed mastery and technique as she moved the objects to optimize mouthing. Her contented glances at me revealed a positive disposition and she played with focus and engagement – I would suggest moderate to high involvement (Laevers *et al.* 1997). Offering this type of play for children older than 12 months of age represents a departure from Goldschmied's original concept, but without any changes to the actual objects the same resource can effectively be enjoyed and developed by babies through to 6-year-olds and older. What differs is how the resource is used. Take this example.

> 'It's a shield' said the 9-year-old boy. 'Yes, and you can use it like this!' said a 6-year-old, demonstrating great technique with a circular-shaped loofah pad looped over his hand, using it to 'bat' other objects. He rummages in the basket before selecting a round massage 'disc', complete with looped handle, which he swiftly secures over his other hand and deftly uses it to bat more objects.

There's nothing unusual about this intergalactic game other than the source of inspiration – a loofah pad, not a typical toy of choice for most 6- or 9-year-olds! Over the course of an hour the two boys played alongside several younger children and babies, each exploring the Treasure Basket and playing in a way that was appropriate to their age and development, creating stories, making up a treasure hunt game, fashioning a padlock from a length of chain, domestic role-play, sound making and more.

Learning points

With examples like these it is easy to make the case for Treasure Baskets being made available to older children.

- Note children's creativity, imagination, concentration, problem solving, social and communication skills.
- The ability of children aged 12 months to 9 years to play happily with the same resource is also noteworthy, especially given that research suggests that mixed-age play is declining (Papatheodorou 2010: 18).

Rules

- Adult supervision is needed during play.
- Do not intervene, prompt, offer resources or suggest uses for objects but instead watch how the child plays.
- There are no right or wrong ways of playing with a Treasure Basket. The aim is to understand rather than judge play, to avoid missing its potential.

Stage 2 – Combining resources

In this stage the Treasure Basket (or a selection of the objects) is offered next to another resource such as sand, water, magnets or mirrors. The children choose whether to use the resources together in their play or not, something that most children typically do. The Continuum generally, and this stage in particular, was inspired by observing children combining resources during play observations. It also drew upon practitioners' comments about children's tendency to use the objects in different parts of the setting and the tidying-up problems that this generated. Instinctively feeling that the answer lay not in restricting this behaviour but providing a mechanism to facilitate this, I offered containers of sand or water near the Treasure Basket to see what

Figure 5.1 Combining resources ensures hands-on learning through play

happened. It was from children's excitement and deep levels of engagement that the idea was born. The second stage of the Continuum was found to be the most highly creative stage of play in observations (Papatheodorou 2010), a factor no doubt linked to its greater 'affordance'. Children typically love to pour, transport, make patterns and engage in role-play, so by combining different media with objects from the basket the level of 'play affordance' or potential (Gibson 1979) significantly increases. Norén-Björn recognizes that 'Loose materials are of crucial significance in enriching play' (cited by Brown 2009: 222); by combining the resources it further extends the appeal and play potential of the Treasure Basket objects as well as magnifying problem-solving opportunities. As with Stage 1, direct adult involvement during play is not desirable, unless of course the **child** engages the **adult** through challenging questions, but the adult still has an important facilitative role to play, as will become apparent in Chapter 9.

What to do

Selecting objects

First decide whether to offer the whole basket of objects for a child to pick from or just a selection which will not be damaged. This will only really apply if offering next to water or some other messy material. If using the same Treasure Basket that babies are accessing, and they are not yet playing with sand, then it may be sensible to use separate objects, to avoid cross-contamination. If using a selection of objects rather than the whole basket, make sure that these offer a good mix not just in terms of appearance and properties but also different functions. The selection of objects set out in Table 5.1 works well.

Selecting play resources

As with the almost limitless potential of the objects themselves, the only limitation on the resources offered alongside the Treasure Basket is our own imagination. If new to this stage of play, try initially offering a Treasure Basket (or collection of objects) next to sand. Next time, explore children's responses to combining objects with water, preferably outside to minimize mess and stress. From here the options are endless as Table 5.2 shows. More sensory play ideas can be found in Lindon *et al.* 2001, Hughes 2009, Featherstone and Williams 2009 and Usher 2010.

Play

Simply provide the selected resource inside or outdoors for a child or group of children to play with. If needed, first agree some general ground rules about play with sand or water so that the play itself can be free from adult intervention. Sit nearby to observe what children play with and how. Children

Table 5.1 The affordance of objects

Suggested objects	Benefits and appeal
A range of spoons, e.g. a metal teaspoon, a large metal spoon, wooden spoon, miniature metal and wooden scoops.	Few children can resist the appeal of transporting objects, sand or water and given that most sand trays come supplied with plastic shapes and utensils, wooden and metal alternatives are very compelling. Another aspect that adds appeal and interest is the range of different shaped tools for scooping offering choice, fine motor skills and problem-solving opportunities and countering functional fixedness (Brown and Kane 1989 cited in Goswami 2002: 287).
Objects with interesting 'profiles', i.e. those that would be good for making imprints in sand, such as a large rubber plug and a lemon reamer.	Most children are obsessed with detail so including profiled objects is great for exploring patterns and making imprints in sand, clay, etc. Children will enjoy the cause and effect satisfaction of making imprints and in many observations, their facial expression at the lack of a pattern indicated their complex thinking and understanding, like the 3-year-old boy who literally did a double take when a rubber plug did not leave an imprint in a pot of dry sand.
Objects that may float or change in water, e.g. a cork coaster and large rubber plug.	By including such objects the adult is not prescribing play itself but providing the possibility for such concepts to be explored if the child so desires.
Objects with a handle that can be used as a tool, e.g. spoons and honey dipper.	These are good for mathematical mark-making or children that are tactile defensive (don't like touching certain materials like sand) and are likely to appeal to those for whom a pencil would not.
A variety of containers, e.g. miniature terracotta flower pot, miniature cardboard box, miniature jam jar, a small tin with lid.	Most children at some point in their childhood enjoy exploring enclosure so this resource provides a wealth of play opportunities. Offering several different types of containers, in terms of size, shape, properties, transparency, with and without lids, different opening mechanisms, etc. all adds to the appeal and potential for problem solving.
Some treasure-like objects, such as a miniature terracotta flower pot, a chain, treasure chest shaped cardboard box or a smooth cobblestone help add interest to would-be treasure hunters.	Countless play sessions have been sparked simply by burying a smooth cobblestone and a few treasure-like objects in sand and providing an eclectic assortment of household brushes and spoons for children to explore. Although straying into Stage 3 of the Continuum (as we shall discover later), if the objects are simply left there with no introduction, children will choose whether to extend the 'play theme' or ignore it. This will of course largely depend upon their ability to recognize that the objects are 'buried treasure', which is more likely in older children, more conversant with pretend play.

Table 5.2 Resources for combining with Treasure Basket objects

Dried rice, lentils, pea shingle	Pastry, clay, etc.
Dried couscous	Mirrors
A mix of dried sand, rice, lentils, etc.	Magnets
Different coloured sand	Magnifying glasses
Sand with glitter, sequins or beads	Soil, leaves, grass and seedpods
Sand mixed with washing-up liquid, powder paint, fruity tea leaves, cinnamon powder, or simply water	Small-world play vehicles and people
	Plasticine or scented play dough in a range of colours
Water with glitter, bubbles, food colouring, ice cubes, pea shingle, sequins	Jelly
	Gloop (I once had to clean up after someone accidentally mixed Treasure Basket objects with gloop. This should only be offered if you are prepared for children to make the inevitable mess and respond positively!)
Recycling resources, e.g. packing 'peanuts'	
Junk modelling containers such as empty cream, yoghurt or margarine pots and plastic fruit trays	Dolls or trucks
	Shaving foam (for sensitive skin)
Snow	

Note: As with all play resources check allergies first and clean objects carefully after use.

typically love combining resources so be prepared for some deeply focused or highly imaginative play. Plan sufficient time for this to take place in an unhurried way or this may destroy the sensory experience that you are creating, not to mention giving children mixed cues.

Sensory-rich play resources each have their own distinct properties or ways of 'behaving' for children to explore and enjoy. Given time, children discover through their own independent learning that sand poured into a sieve will naturally flow through the holes, unless of course water is added to the sand to change its consistency, as the children in Chapter 6 discover! The appeal for children lies perhaps in the countless opportunities and challenges provided by such simple resources, particularly when combined with their own bodies, or another object or resource such as water:

> Z (2 years and 2 months) picked up the metal square bowl and held
> it with both hands and put it in to his mouth and tilted it as if he

were drinking it. Z dropped it and it splashed. Z bent down and was using his hands to splash it in to the water . . . C (2 years and 4 months) then picked up the leather sponge and was squeezing it. 'What is it C?' 'I don't know', said C. 'What does it do?' C dropped it and it went splash. 'Splash', C said. C picked it up and was tapping the sponge using his left hand and then squeezing it. 'I'm watering.'

In a separate observation a child uses the objects with a mixture of dried sand, couscous and rice:

He picks up the tea strainer and takes it to the sand tray. He scoops up the sand and holds it over a metal spatula to sprinkle. The sand and rice mixture doesn't come through the holes. He picks up the metal spoon and holds the large swirly shaped shell steady whilst he pours the sand into the 'mouth' of the shell. He looks surprised that the mixture doesn't come through the holes.

Learning points

The children can be seen demonstrating:

- 'What can I do with it?' Pressing the egg cup, dropping the objects in water and scooping sand. 'What can this become?' 'I'm watering', trying to use the scrunchie as a bracelet, pretending to drink from the cup, and so on.
- Transforming and trajectory schemas may also be apparent in the first observation as they transform the springy egg cup and drop the objects in water to change the water and object.
- The second observation suggests that the child is testing concepts and ideas and that he is surprised by the mixture not coming through the holes. He then moves to a larger hole, the mouth of the shell, possibly to continue testing his thoughts.
- A range of typical Treasure Basket behaviours such as two-handed holding, manipulation, transporting, problem solving, creativity, language and pretend play are also apparent (see Chapter 4).
- High levels of engagement such as these are typically seen at this stage of play, but are best appreciated via a fuller observation, as we shall see in Chapter 6.

Rules

- Critical to the success of this approach is the provision of the objects next to rather than 'in' the sand, water or other medium: that way there is less scope for children to misinterpret object position as a cue for using any or particular objects in play.

- Once you have checked and provided the resources, the adult's role is simply to observe play to inform future planning; provide a reassuring presence if needed; and only to intervene to ensure safety.
- The choice of objects, resources and location should be based upon the practitioner's knowledge of the particular child or children's likes, dislikes and interests. This does not mean, however, that children should only be offered what they are used to. The trick is to help nudge children towards the Zone of Proximal Development (ZPD), where learning is extended beyond what they would achieve through independent play (Vygotsky 1978: 85), using observations to inform your selection.

Stage 3 – Adult-initiated play

The final stage of the Continuum involves using simple, adult-initiated activities with Treasure Basket objects. Many activities may be inspired by children themselves, others may fit well with a topic or focus, but in choosing which activity to use it is important to consider and be led by the child's interests and developmental levels. The success or otherwise of this third stage is dependent upon the skill of the practitioner in picking an appropriate activity which captures children's interest and a facilitative approach which encourages their ownership of the process. Where this has worked well, children have quickly taken ownership of the adult-initiated activity, turning it into a joint or child-led activity instead. In this third stage, the adult's role is clearly more proactive, selecting activities based on children's interests and abilities and supporting or extending children's questions, discovery and thinking. Through support and facilitation, the adult's skill and sensitivity, particularly from building upon children's interests and developmental levels, can help children to move to the ZPD.

What to do

Selecting activity
First decide which child or children to invite to play, then select an appropriate activity for their age, interests and needs. This requires insight and skill if the activity is quickly to become child led. Prepare the resources needed together with the appropriate environment for play. Ideally introduce the Treasure Basket on the floor, as with the other stages, rather than at tables – as we shall discover in Chapter 9 this can indicate work rather than play to children. Before launching into an activity, give time to initially explore the objects

otherwise children may be distracted during play as their minds are elsewhere. Introduce the activity in a simple and upbeat way and be prepared to change tack or emphasis if children's interest takes them in a different direction. Although this is **adult initiated** this does not mean it should be **adult led**. If you have chosen well, children should engage with the activity, adding their own ideas and shaping the direction of play in the activity and subsequently. The range of activities that can be played with a Treasure Basket is endless, so let your imagination flow and have fun. Table 5.3 contains some popular activities to get you started. For more curriculum-linked activity ideas see also Hughes 2009 and Playscope Activity Cards (www.playtoz.co.uk).

Play

Some activities can be as simple as talking about the objects. The following observation of some 2-year-olds reveals a further potential benefit of Stage 3, as a child who might not otherwise have contributed seems to find a voice through play.

> The children first familiarized themselves with the Treasure Basket as many had not seen it before. Looking through the objects, the children identify ones that they know. Child 4 (2 years and 2 months) is not very chatty at this point, observing friends and their reactions, although the child does feel the loofah when it is passed round. Child 1 (2 years and 6 months) becomes excited and recognizes the whisk, doing circular whisking motions with arms. 'It do that', Child 1 whispers. Child 1 identifies the shell item as a 'circle' and the orange as the shape of a 'ball'.
>
> (Gascoyne 2010)

Learning points

- Child 1 is normally quiet in this type of activity so it was felt that perhaps working in a smaller group or engaging with objects gave more opportunities for this child to be heard.
- It is interesting how this activity begins with what is familiar and relevant to the children, giving opportunities for them to be 'experts' and make the links with home.
- Children naturally, without any prompting, relate the objects to mathematical shapes.
- In the fuller observation Child 4, initially quiet, takes on a much more proactive role. This is a helpful reminder of children's different learning styles, indicative perhaps of this child's need for reflection time, and the importance of adults not rushing this.

Table 5.3 Treasure Basket activities

Activity ideas	Benefits	Example
In the balance Children take it in turns picking two objects and pretend that their arms are an old-fashioned set of balancing scales to try to work out which object is heavier. They then check using a set of scales and talk about any surprises.	Great for problem solving, developing thinking skills and honing predictions.	In a session with approximately seven 4-year-olds the children eagerly picked objects and guessed weights. After several turns each the play naturally evolved into a musical session with children selecting objects to make different sounds and picking tunes to play and sing. Some children then returned to weighing objects on their own.
Sink or swim Children guess which of the objects will sink and which will float in water. Increase interest by adding glitter, sequins or bubbles to the water. Introduce language by writing 'sink' or 'swim' on little cards for older children to use to recreate 3D tables.	Great for problem solving, developing thinking skills and honing predictions.	In one session three children aged 4 years and 6 months to 4 years and 9 months explored the objects, talking about what they were made of and whether they thought they would sink or swim. Interestingly, one of the children only picked metal objects and similarly showed a preference for metal in previous sessions. Some of the objects behaved differently to the children's expectations, which introduced opportunities for discussion and extending learning.
Buried treasure Hide some of the treasure-like objects in dried sand in a tray. Provide a selection of different brushes and spoons nearby for the children to use for a mini-archaeological dig. Extend by providing magnets and adapting what is buried for a foray into metal detecting.	Great for hand–eye co-ordination, fine motor skills and imagination. Develops problem solving and thinking skills.	This type of activity has been known to engage children for hours. Introduce by simply saying you've heard that a fossilized dinosaur egg is buried and watch the children use the tools and develop their own play such as re-burying objects for others to find, making patterns in the sand, for domestic role-play, etc.
Story making Children can pick objects from the basket to create their own 'silly' stories; use several objects to weave a story; create sound stories from the noises made by the objects; or play a variation of 'My grandmother went to the shop and bought . . .' in which they try to remember the different objects.	Great for honing listening and memory skills, for encouraging creativity, divergent thinking and imagination. Develops language and personal, social and emotional skills.	Sound making appeals to most children and this activity enables babies and young children to be involved in their own way, e.g. by picking objects and making a sound; saying what they think it sounds like; or finding sounds to reflect particular animals or actions.

Rules

- The aim is for children to take ownership of the activity, rather than the adult retaining tight control, so think carefully about how best to create an enabling environment by keeping the activity playful and fun and offering opportunities for choice. (See Chapter 9 for more ideas.)
- Provide adequate time and opportunities for children to revisit the activity without adult involvement, as numerous observations have revealed high levels of engagement and 'compositional' play (where the child adds to the play) when children have re-enacted or returned to and modified play (Papatheodorou 2010).
- Observe subsequent play for signs of play or learning being extended and support if needed.

In this chapter we have explored the three Stages of the Continuum, witnessing protracted periods of deeply focused exploration and play in Stages 1 and 2 and, in the hands of a skilled facilitator, the potential for creative and compositional play in Stage 3. So far just a taster has been provided of children's responses to play at each of the stages. In the next chapter we will follow children through all three stages to gain a better insight into the special appeal of play, the dance-like qualities of interaction between child, adult and resources, its benefits for older children and its implications for the adult's role.

6 The Sensory Play Continuum in action

The continuum of sensory play functions in multiple cycles of actions, . . the experience from stage three is internalised to lead to free play and play with [a] combination of other materials and resources.

(Papatheodorou, *Sensory Play*)

Overview

In Chapter 5 we introduced the Sensory Play Continuum as a framework for offering and increasing play opportunities for children across the ages. In this chapter we will follow three children on their journey along the Continuum to gain a deeper insight into children's play in each of the three stages and identify features, characteristics and qualitative differences in play.

Child S – Stage 1

Context

S (aged 8 months) has had access to Treasure Baskets on a few occasions. The baby room does a lot of sensory-type play, but generally using one type of resource at a time or during sensory play sessions and in a more adult-directed way than free play with the Treasure Basket. The practitioner sits down with the Treasure Basket and invites S over; she freely comes and plays without adult intervention. Another Treasure Basket is set up for other children to investigate.

S starts by emptying objects one at a time until she finds the metal teaspoon. She starts mouthing this, then picks up the measuring spoon and starts mouthing that. She shows the spoon to another staff member, offers it to her, then takes it back laughing several times. S returns to emptying objects one at a time and mouthing the metal objects. S comes over to me [she was distracted by the flash of the camera]. She then goes to investigate what another member of staff was doing, then returns to the Treasure Basket where she starts emptying all the fabric items. She doesn't just take the top object but rummages in the basket. S comes over to me, goes to another staff member then returns to the Treasure Basket. She picks up the metal bucket, starts balancing the handle on her fingers, babbling and looking inside. She then starts to dance to music, playing on a toy that another child is playing with. S leaves 'her' Treasure Basket and joins children at another basket. She chooses the pan and shows it to another child before leaving the activity to go to the construction toys.

- Child S appears to have a preference for playing with the metal objects – possibly because of their coldness or shininess.
- Typical play behaviours include picking up, placing, manipulation, babbling, exploring and mouthing objects and showing objects to others.
- The session lasts 25 minutes but there are a number of distractions, e.g. camera flash and musical toys in close proximity which may have disturbed her concentration. This has important implications for the adults' role in providing an enabling environment.

Child S – Stage 2

The practitioner sets up the sand tray and a shallow tray with purple coloured sand and adds items from the Treasure Basket.

S starts at the shallow tray and starts spooning sand using the teaspoon. She puts the handle end in her mouth and discovers that the sand is stuck to the wet part of the spoon, and continues spooning sand and putting the handle end in her mouth. She transfers from one tray to another, continuing using the teaspoon. The practitioner adds brushes; she looks at these, discards them and continues using the teaspoon, holding the spoon end and spooning with the handle end. S ignores other children crawling through the sand tray and continues spooning. S attempts to spoon around another child sitting in the sand tray and then moves away.

Learning points

- The child's apparent preference for metal objects appears to be reinforced.
- She displays great focus and concentration, probably 'extremely high' involvement (Laevers *et al.* 1997), e.g. when continuing to spoon the sand around the crawling and seated child.
- She mouths, transports, manipulates and turns the objects with her hands. She appears to have made a link between the stuck sand and wetness.
- The practitioner sensitively adds objects, which are ignored without interrupting play.
- The session lasts about thirty minutes. Play is cut short by another child's presence.

Child S – Stage 3

Context

Most of the babies are sleeping, with one being fed, so the practitioner gets the Treasure Basket out and invites Child S over.

Observation

I [the practitioner] put the crocheted mat on my head, saying 'I'm putting my hat on.' S watches and smiles. I pretend to sneeze and let the cloth fall off my head into S's lap. She chuckles [her chuckles are more like anticipation of something funny about to happen] then hands me the cloth. I repeat the activity again. S chuckles as I put the cloth on my head and really laughs when it falls off [S's laughs are real belly laughs]. S then picks up the cloth with two hands and puts it on her own head, looking at me as she does so. S lets go of the crochet cloth and it falls off. She snorts [screws her nose up and breathes quick and heavy] and laughs. I repeat the action of putting it on my head and dropping it. S laughs. S looks in the Treasure Basket which is next to her and picks out the metal spoon; she mouths it and smiles at me. She looks back in the basket and gets the tea strainer and drops the spoon. She mouths this and then gets the tea ball, shakes it and lets the chain swing. She drops this and crawls away.

Learning points

- The observation reveals the gentle way in which the child modifies play from the activity to free play and then crawls away to signal the session end after about 25 minutes.
- The child's repeated preference for metal objects is evident and her smile at the practitioner may be indicative of her recognition of the teaspoon that she has played with previously.
- Child S immediately engaged in turn-taking and mimicking the adult. The session is indicative of a conversation as she first gives the mat to the practitioner to repeat then puts the mat on her head and actively joins in the play, which is now no longer adult led.
- This playful activity, and the different permutations of laughter evoked, gives an insight into the child's personality.
- Typical behaviours include placing, dropping, looking to the carer, two-handed play, exploration, communication, mouthing and manipulation.

Child R – Stage 1

Context

R (aged 2 years and 1 month) wakes from his sleep and is invited over to the book area where he likes to play. He is asked if he would like to play with the Treasure Basket. This is the first time he has played with this particular Treasure Basket in the setting, but he has previously had access to baskets of collections of objects made from the same materials. Child R enjoys books and spends a lot of time reading to himself or being read to in the book corner. Staff were keen to help him integrate with other children and resources.

Observation

R picks up objects one at a time, looks at them, waves them and places them next to himself. He chats to himself while doing this.

Words are mainly unrecognizable, but occasionally words such as 'ball' are heard. All his chatter is very animated, with a range of intonation. He then moves on to playing with objects together. He picks up the pan, puts the metal whisk in the pan and then tries other metal objects together. He tries to put the wooden whisk into the pan; this doesn't fit. He returns to emptying and investigating objects one at a time.

Two other children join and R leaves the Treasure Basket then quickly returns and continues emptying objects one at a time. He then starts reading the miniature book to himself. When he finishes reading the book he says, 'Bye bye book' and continues emptying objects one at a time from the basket; each time he chats to himself. Another child joins, there is no interaction between the children. R continues investigating objects and placing them next to himself. R returns to the book, puts it back in the Treasure Basket when he has finished reading it, then puts the other objects back in the basket, chatting to himself. R leaves the activity and goes to play in the home corner.

Learning points

- The following typical play behaviours are seen: picking up, placing, waving, sorting, verbalizing, using two objects together, putting an object inside another and generally exploring objects.
- Play changes from single-item exploration to playing with objects together. Problem solving and trial and error are evident as he tries to put objects in the pan.
- Although non-social, R is very vocal during the session, as is typical of his play generally. He speaks to the book and appears to give an inner commentary on the objects and his actions.
- The session lasts about 25 minutes.

Child R – Stage 2

Context

The session was observed by an experienced nursery practitioner. The practitioner opened the sand tray and placed the Treasure Basket containing most of the objects (except the fabric objects, cardboard box, book, rush mat and loofah) next to the sand tray. There were no other resources in the sand, but these were in the usual containers next to the sand where they could be freely accessed as usual. Child C (aged 2 years and 8 months) very rarely plays in the sand tray, preferring the mark-making area and small-world where he typically plays without commentary or communication with others. He has good vocabulary and willingly talks to adults when they initiate conversation, or to seek approval from adults.

Observation

Three children come to the sand tray. R chooses the pan, metal egg cup and wooden spoon. He tries filling both the pan and egg cup with sand using the wooden spoon. Child B (2 years and 2 months) then empties all the objects out of the Treasure Basket into the sand tray. R puts the peg into the pan, then picks up the tin and attempts to place it on top of the objects in the pan. He plays in silence, not attempting to communicate with anyone or to make any utterances during his play. Child B says, while unscrewing the top from the jar, 'Open the door' – then moves on to filling the wooden egg cup and jar, and gets the whisk, saying 'Mixing it.' R then gets the whisk and says, 'Mix, mix' several times.

Child C joins the other two children at the sand tray. He attempts to fill the metal egg cup several times before choosing the jar to fill. R gets the jar, attempts to put the whisk inside, abandons the whisk when it does not fit, then tries the tin lid before finding the jar lid, and successfully puts it on top of the jar. He then gets the pan and brush, saying, 'Mixing.' After about 20 minutes R leaves the sand tray and goes to play with the construction toys. Child C spends 10 minutes filling a small metal bowl and half a tea ball using the teaspoon. After filling he smoothes the sand, pats it, then uses the brush to brush the sand. He does this very carefully with good fine motor control.

Child C's play then changes to pretend play and he starts commenting on his own play. He fills the metal egg cup with sand and says, 'Wait a minute, need egg.' He fills the pan with sand saying, 'Making tea now.' He continues filling the tin with sand, shows it to me saying, 'Sand inside of it, see.' There is no interaction between the children. Child C continues filling the tin – 'Lots of sand in there, but we not need more, put lid on so not broke' then piles sand on top of the tin with the lid on. He fills the jar saying, 'That enough of sand in there but we patting it, we put it there, now we pat it yes.' Child C shows Child B his tin saying, 'Sand in it, look.' They continue to play alongside one another. Child C uses the whisk – 'just mixing that sand, now it's ready'. He continues opening the tin, emptying and filling it and then placing the lid back, then puts more sand on top of the closed tin – 'That enough sand on there, but me patting it. That enough.' Child B leaves, Child C gets the pastry brush and starts brushing the sand off the sides of the sand tray and off his hands repeating, 'Brush, brush, brush', then singing, 'Brush, brush, brush it off, it clean now, it not got any sand on it anymore.' He looks at several objects, cleans them with his brush, commenting on what he is doing and singing, 'brush, brush, brush it off.' He cleans the edge of the sand tray, puts sand back on the edge and cleans it off again, cleaning several objects saying, 'There's no sand in it now.' Child C starts burying objects, saying, 'Where's it gone?' then finding it, saying, 'Here it is.' This continues for about ten minutes before the rest of the children start tidying up the other areas of the room. He cleans the toys with the brush before putting them back in the basket.

Learning points

- R's play is normally very vocal, as in Stage 1, but the addition of sand appears to have changed this, as he plays almost in silence, possibly a sign of concentration.
- R picks up, fills, combines objects and balances, commentates and engages in pretend play. He seemingly resumes his exploration of what fits what as he tries putting the whisk in the jar and successfully finds the jar lid and puts this on.
- Child C does not normally choose to play with sand yet plays with focus for over an hour.
- Child C's play – filling the tin with a spoon, smoothing the top and how he uses the brush in the sand – is reminiscent of Child Z at Stage 2 (see separate observation).
- Child C's play appears to evolve to pretend play, showing a progression from 'What is this object like?' and 'What can I do with it?' to 'What can it become?'
- Child C appears to invent his own game of hiding the objects, which may have continued had tidying up not distracted him. This game is reminiscent of the buried treasure activity suggested in Chapter 5, itself inspired by a child's play. He contentedly merges the activity and task of tidying up by using the pastry brush for this.
- Child C generally plays quietly, but during this activity was very vocal, commenting on his own play and initiating conversations with the adult and peers.

Child R – Stage 3

Context

Due to R's interest in books an activity involving a story was picked. The practitioner used a colourful large poster to remind the children of the story. After the children had finished their snack, I asked them if they would like to listen to the story of the 'Three Little Pigs'. We read the story using toy pigs and a wolf as props. Afterwards I introduced the Treasure Basket and suggested that we find objects for building the three pigs' houses. Two other children listened to the story but did not stay for the activity.

Observation

All the children joined in with the 'huff, puff and blow your house down' and enjoyed blowing during the story. R starts helping me sort the objects from the basket for the house building, but quickly returns to the story poster and starts retelling the story in his own words. He points to all the pigs, naming them, and shows me that the wolf has fallen down. He repeats 'bang' and claps at the picture of the wooden house falling down. He starts playing with the Treasure Basket as he did in Stage 1 – getting the pan and whisk, saying, 'Mix, mix.' He then places the felt teddy on top of the loofah, saying, 'Night, night' and points to the picture of the wolf lying on the floor at the end of the story. He then finds the mini book in the basket and starts reading it, naming objects in the pictures. He then hands it to me to read to him. He returns to the story poster, pointing to pictures, retelling the story to himself before leaving the area.

Learning points

- Practitioners were aware of the activity's potential age limitations (being targeted at 3-year-olds upwards) but it was picked because of R's interest in books. R (and his two peers) quickly lost interest in sorting the objects (possibly because the objects were not similar enough to what they were supposed to represent – building materials – and therefore not relevant to them. However, R's focus on books appears to sustain his interest in the story and objects some time after the first reading. Although the activity was not age-appropriate it is interesting that he does not use the toy pigs and wolf to re-enact the story but instead selects objects from the Treasure Basket. His play with the Treasure Basket appears to change compared to the previous sessions as he seems to link his play with the story, suggesting that the juxtaposition of the story and objects offer some value. This points to the potential compositional value of play at this stage and the importance of the 'figures' being sufficiently open-ended to facilitate play.

- R develops play in several ways, by
  - retelling the story using the poster;
  - repeating his previous mixing behaviour;
  - linking the objects to the story, re-enacting and evolving it;
  - shifting focus to the mini book but in a social capacity;
  - retelling the story using the poster again.
- The adult responds flexibly, allowing Child R to take ownership and control.
- The session lasts about 35 minutes.

Child Z – Stage 1

Context

This observation with a three-and-a-half-year-old took place in a family home. His Treasure Basket, with which he had played for over two years, was simply put on a rug on the floor. I sat nearby, videoing play. The session lasted over an hour and was cut short by a distraction from an older sibling. There is no adult involvement. (Due to the observation being videoed rather than written notes, the actions take the form of bullet points.)

Observation

- Z picks a small tin bucket, measuring cup with handle, metal 'choke' chain, piece of cloth and wooden scoop and concentrates intently as he plays with these.
- He attempts to coil the heavy chain into the small bucket. On succeeding he uses the scoop to mix the chain in the bucket, then scoop the contents and transfer the chain to a second pot. He repeats this a second time.
- He manoeuvres the handle of the bucket and uses the wooden scoop to move the chain within the pot as though 'folding' a cake mix. He then takes hold of the chain in the fingers of one hand and extends his arm straight up into the air so that the chain is extended at full length. He holds the measuring pot by its handle in the other hand; holding it still he tries to line the chain up with the pot to fill it. This requires considerable effort as the chain is heavy and about 60 cm long, with the end of the chain swaying like a pendulum.

- He manages to get the end of the chain in the pot but several times finds that it quickly snakes out due to the weight of the chain hanging out of the pot. After several attempts he succeeds in getting enough of the chain in it for it not to fall out. A look of satisfaction spreads across his face.
- He uses the wooden lemon zester with the pot in a similar way to using a pestle and mortar.
- His older sister has decided to take pictures of her brother playing and the camera flash momentarily distracts him.
- He adjusts his position relative to the basket. He then 'tosses' the pan with the chain in it and when it falls out he slides the pot sideways along the floor to scoop up the chain. He repeats the tossing action numerous times and on one 'failed' occasion reaches for the cream cloth and wipes up a 'spillage'. He continues tossing the chain until he manages to toss it 23 times without the chain falling out. He repeats, making even more pronounced actions, and manages to bang his knee, which he clasps with both hands.
- [With the benefit of a different angle I spot that throughout his play] he has been positioning a small spoon, juicer, bucket, scoop, pot brush, large metal spoon and cloth in a line, as he does with lots of his toys.
- His sister whispers loudly to me 'What's he doing?' Before I can answer but after a pause he turns to us and says emphatically, 'I'm doing something, it's something tricky.'

Learning points

- Play involves just five items from the basket and these appear to be used for experimentation, problem solving and domestic role-play.
- He concentrates intently for an hour (extremely high involvement, Laevers *et al.* 1997), apparently focused on a self-set challenge.
- He shows accomplished fine motor skills as he manipulates the chain and at no point appears frustrated when the chain falls out.
- A number of possible schema are apparent: lining up (as he lines up the objects?), rotation (mixing?), trajectory (tossing the chain?), transforming (manipulating the chain?).
- He plays in silence with the exception of his comment at the end. This perfectly conveys the essence of play as 'child's work'.
- The camera flash did not appear to distract his play; he simply repositioned himself to enable concentration. However, the impact of the observer and camera use are highlighted as challenges for adults to address.

Child Z – Stage 2

At Stage 2 of the Sensory Play Continuum, Child Z was observed playing outside with a shallow sledge filled with sand, a toy cement mixer and dumper truck. The toys had inadvertently been found in the sand during set-up and as the boy had been asking about these lost toys in the preceding week the Treasure Basket was left some distance away on the assumption that it would not be used by the child. The observation lasted nearly an hour (interrupted again) and was videoed. This is a summary of the full observation.

Z sits and starts playing with the truck, cement mixer and sand. After less than a minute he asks if he can get the Treasure Basket and uses the spoons and pots to fill the truck and mixer. Throughout his play Z uses the toys less and less. He uses several of the spoons, brushes and pots from the basket to fill and transfer sand to the toys but the time interval between using the toys increases each time. He fills and transfers sand from one container to another, smoothes the sand to close the box lid, uses the plug to make an imprint in the sand in a bucket, wipes up sand spillages and repeats similar actions. He stands up and uses the rope on the sledge to pull the objects in a circle around the mat. He repeats, then fills a pot, at first while holding the rope, then picks up the rope and carefully manoeuvres the sledge while holding a pot in his other hand. He continues playing with the objects and sand (in a different position) and discards the truck which he has been scooping around onto the grass. He stands, stoops over the sledge, fills a pot with sand and goes to put some sand in the truck. He stops, looks at his wellington boots nearby and pours the sand into one boot instead. He resumes play, scooping sand with a metal spoon. After some time he stands to pull the sledge again, goes over to his boots and puts his foot in one boot. He pauses, looks down and tips up the boot full of sand.

- Given Z's interest in the toys it is surprising that he chooses to use the Treasure Basket objects with them. Z touched the two plastic toys just 11 times in 55 minutes, and only then in conjunction with the objects. Z insisted on taking some of the Treasure Basket objects in the bath to continue his play, leaving the toys in the sand.

- He reveals focus, fine motor skills, problem solving and creativity.
- Throughout his play he hums or makes 'singsong' noises.
- He explores transporting (sand and objects on small and large scale), enclosure (putting sand in objects), rotation (cement mixer, mixing in pot and rotation of sledge).
- It appears to be a conscious decision to put the sand in his boot rather than the truck and he looks surprised when he puts the boot on.
- The session was truncated by his older sister calling loudly in the garden but he insisted on taking three wooden utensils into the house and in his bath later that day!

Child Z – Stage 3

Context

At Stage 3 of the Sensory Play Continuum, Child Z is observed playing inside with his older sister present (aged 6 years). In this session Z and his sister play a game of guessing which objects from the Treasure Basket would be attracted to a magnet. The session came about when a large box arrived in the post and the children discovered the magnets inside. The key points from the observation are summarized below.

Observation

- I suggested we explore the Treasure Basket objects with the magnets. The children each held a large horseshoe magnet and experimented with hovering this over the basket to see what happened.
- They then sorted through the objects to see if they could find items to use with the magnets, predicting first whether they thought the object would attract or not. On several occasions they were surprised to discover that the magnets didn't attract to some of the metal items.
- With the basket now empty I put some objects in it and covered these with a 'magic cloth'. The children were invited to guess whether the hidden objects would be attracted to the magnets. This introduced surprise and excitement as they held the magnet and sometimes the cloth lifted like a magician's act. The 6-year-old took the lead in positioning some objects on the floor under the cloth and

inviting her sibling to guess what would happen, building to a crescendo of excitement as the cloth lifted.

- They took it in turns hiding the objects before the 6-year-old began exploring weight and attraction by using two magnets for the heavy items. This was sparked by an object falling from the magnet.
- Child Z explored how many different objects he could pick up with one magnet.

Learning points

- The excitement at discovering the magnets sparked play and the activity built upon their eagerness to try out the magnets.
- Play evolved with the children taking the lead, e.g. using the cloth to cover the objects and introduce excitement; exploring weight; using two magnets to see if they would work on heavier objects; seeing how many objects they could pick up with the magnet.
- The range of objects allowed the older sibling to test her theories and question why the magnet only worked with some of the metal objects. Z benefited from copying his sister.
- The observer took a more active role than usual to enable Z to contribute, explore and discover without the older sibling doing this all for him.
- The session lasted about 45 minutes.

Common themes to emerge

Stage 1

- Sorting featured in several of the sessions. At first sight this may appear random, but given our knowledge of the significance of objects *per se*, and hand movements in particular, this is unlikely to be the case.
- A preference for metal objects was evident in several of the sessions.
- There is evidence of heuristic play behaviours – i.e. exploring what they can do with the objects and 'scientific experimentation' as a precursor to moving onto domestic play.
- Domestic role-play was present in several of the sessions and is believed to be a first stage in pretend play, making a transition between the world of fantasy and everyday life (Garvey 1986: 47).
- The impact upon language is noteworthy, with some children vocalizing who were not typically vocal in play, while other normally

vocal children played in silence. This is an area for further investigation.

Stage 2

- Children are seen exploring 'What is this like?', 'What can I do with this?' and 'What can this become?'
- Heuristic play behaviours are apparent as children explore, try, repeat and refine what they can do with the objects and undergo a process of scientific discovery.
- There is evidence of compositional play, where the objects take on greater significance as children create something which is greater than its parts (Papatheodorou 2010). An example of this is the teddy and loofah being used by Child R to represent the wolf in bed. Not only did the child use an object to symbolize a character in the story but the loofah adds an extra stage to the story.
- Evidence suggests that the juxtaposition of resources and/or peers can help children reach the zone of proximal development (ZPD). Although not evident in these particular observations, it is apparent in the children discovering the properties of sand and mathematics in Chapter 7.
- The presence and use of language is interesting, with changes in typical language use and domination observed across the ages, from babbling through to discussion.

Stage 3

Where children were given sufficient time and freedom to do so, play became child led and characterized by exploring what they can do with the objects, scientific experimentation, problem solving and domestic role-play.

- Does the activity, practitioner, peer or juxtaposition of the resources help take children to the ZPD?
- There was evidence of compositional play (Papatheodorou 2010). In a separate play session, 4- and 5-year-old children built towers from the objects. One group decides 'It's going to be a castle.' Once nearly complete they add, 'We need to put the flag on!' and get a fabric bow from the Treasure Basket to add to the top of their castle. To the surprise of the practitioner the activity lasted for an hour.

- With sensitive facilitation and the right activity this stage yielded insight into children's personality and 'what makes them tick'.
- There was evidence of positive social relations between children and practitioners, like Child S and her different types of laughter.

General points

- Importance of practitioner knowledge and tailoring the offer to suit particular children, factors that we will consider further in Chapter 9.
- Importance of giving children sufficient time and space for play to evolve naturally.
- The prevalence of heuristic play behaviours during play with a Treasure Basket in Stage 1 and 2 of the Continuum – an important revelation where space, time or budgets are constrained and 1- to 2-year-olds are present.
- Heuristic play was developed for children in their second year when focus, sharing and increased mobility may present a challenge. Observations support the value of the Sensory Play Continuum in meeting this age group's needs. Altercations about particular objects were limited and quickly diffused by a child spotting another, equally covetable object.
- Exploration evolved into pretend play in several observations and should perhaps be seen as part of a continuum rather than distinct activities.

Children's involvement and the Continuum

- In Chapter 4 we witnessed children's high levels of engagement when playing freely with a Treasure Basket. Typically I have seen children aged from 6 months to 9 years playing for an hour or more, deeply engaged in exploring the objects, testing their potential and (with the older children) using them for role-play. I would typically position the Treasure Basket free play sessions that I have observed over several years at 'moderate to extremely high involvement' (Laevers *et al.* 1997), with a good proportion of these being at the upper end of this scale. Clearly this lacks rigorous quantification and analysis, being based purely on qualitative observations and with levels of involvement not the only factor being observed. However, it has been possible to apply the Involvement Scale for Young Children (Laevers *et al.* 1997) to video footage of play (*Exploratory*

Play 2006; Papatheodorou 2010), and this appears to concur with this view.

- Papatheodorou (2010) concluded that Stage 2 of the Continuum was the most creative stage of play and the language and behavioural responses outlined certainly seem to suggest high levels of involvement. Analysis of a videoed observation of a 3-year-old playing with sand and objects found involvement at Scale 4 to 5, a factor which also accords with my qualitative assessments of play in numerous sessions at this stage. This goes some way to explaining a 2-year-old boy's play with sand and Treasure Basket objects for three hours!

The Continuum and pretend play

We saw in Chapter 3 that the more similar in appearance two objects are, the greater likelihood there is that they will be categorized together. A relationship has also been found between how representative an object is, children's age, and their ability to engage in pretend play. A young child playing with a Treasure Basket will use the objects for explorative play and then, if ready, progress onto domestic and social re-enactments – a fusion between the child's real world and make-believe. For young children to venture into the world of make-believe play, objects have to be sufficiently realistic-looking to act as an 'anchor' for play (Fein 1975, cited in Garvey 1986: 48). Child R and his peers' reaction in Chapter 6 to using the objects to build houses shows that when objects are too different to the building materials that they are symbolizing, they lack relevance. In contrast, older children will happily use objects that bear little relationship to their symbolic meaning, such as using a metal measuring cup as a telephone, as a 2-year and 10-month-old did in one observation. As children get older it is less important for the scale and appearance of objects to closely match their symbolic meaning. In fact, 'less realistic objects appear to facilitate make-believe play [affording] more scope for inventiveness and imagination, permitting the child to transform them to suit the occasion' (Garvey 1986: 49). The following observation of a 3- to 4-year-old boy seems to illustrate the potential for objects to stifle.

> Repeatedly the boy's domestic role-play never got beyond tipping a basket of play food and plates on the floor. Each time he momentarily paused to look at the toys before walking away. The same aged child played deeply engaged in domestic role-play using the objects from a Treasure Basket. In spontaneous play sessions lasting over an hour (some with sand, others just using the objects on their own) he was

observed repeatedly mixing, tossing a chain in a measuring cup ['spaghetti' perhaps?], and wiping up a 'spillage' with a cloth.

At first sight domestic role-play offered little appeal to this little boy, but other observations point to the importance of open-ended resources as a driver for this boy's creativity.

The Continuum and older children's play

An older child encountering a Treasure Basket, or simply a set of objects, for the first time will almost certainly focus on 'What is this object like?' and 'What can I do with it?' Unlike a baby or toddler whose explorations will last several months, an older child will move through this at an accelerated rate. Perhaps this is because their explorations are adding to an already established set of rules and categories for understanding objects and so exploration simply adds an extra layer of thinking or connections with existing knowledge rather than forming new categories. This speed of transition is evident from the 6- and 9-year-olds' play described in Chapter 4 and the ease with which they were able to use loofah and sisal pads to enter into the world of

Figure 6.1 Sensory-rich resources like these offer age-appropriate play and learning opportunities

intergalactic combat! Interestingly, the belief that older children cannot play with a Treasure Basket in the same way that a baby does, because the former will be drawing upon previous knowledge and experiences and therefore cannot look at it fresh, does not appear to be true as neuroscientists have discovered that even 4-month-olds' categorization will be based upon previous stored knowledge.

Rule acquisition and the Continuum

In Chapter 3 we discovered the importance of category development in children's brains as a tool for decoding the world, developing language and storing and recollecting memories. Using animals to illustrate, categories develop on a global level, e.g. mammals; a basic level, e.g. dogs; and a superordinate level, e.g. collies (Rosch *et al.* 1976, cited in Quinn 2002). How this occurs and in which order is unclear, although evidence points to the fact that exposure to sufficient numbers of basic-level examples leads to representation initially at the global level (Quinn 2002: 100). With limited opportunities for developing and testing rules, children are only able to make very simple distinctions such as between animals and furniture! However, with ample opportunities for exploring properties, shape, movement, colour, function and so much more through Treasure Basket play, infants are able to reuse and refine their thinking at all category levels.

Potential parallels can also be seen between the types of investigations needed to categorize thinking about objects and the type of play behaviours typically associated with the different stages of play in the Sensory Play Continuum. At its simplest the three stages of the Continuum offer three different contexts for play with objects. In Stage 1, the juxtaposition of objects within the basket offers endless permutations for exploring and reframing the objects. (We saw in Chapter 3 that the context of an object shapes its perception and rule acquisition, and this can be seen in action at this stage.) In Stage 2 the context is changed again with the addition of another medium commensurate with a shift in equilibrium as the child encounters how the object 'interacts' with other materials. This is particularly true of highly changeable resources like sand, water and so on, as these have their own innate properties and 'discipline' (Matterson 1975: 42), and when used in conjunction with the objects offer huge potential for discombobulating moments. With a skilled practitioner, the third stage offers another opportunity to reframe the same objects. By making links to interests and topics and offering different ways of using the objects, children's 'views' remain fluid and opportunities for further refinement of categories are increased, known as cognitive flexibility (Brown and Kane 1989, cited in Goswami 2002). This is particularly true when children revisit activities and develop their own take on play, resulting in a compositional type of play. The sum of the three stages helps mediate against functional fixedness and seemingly supports complex categorization.

Play, exploration and the Continuum

The debate about where exploration fits in the world of play has led many to argue that exploration is not play and that 'real' play, in the spirit of Vygotsky, is pretend play where the child 'brings something unique, new and of themself' (1978). The link between familiarization with objects through exploration and problem solving and divergent thinking is compelling (Fein 1975, cited in Garvey 1986; Pepler and Ross 1981). Recent brain mapping research suggests that the brain is characterized by high levels of excitement during explorative play (signified by red colouration in brain scans) whereas during role-play, in this instance pretend cooking with Treasure Basket objects, deep levels of engagement were apparent (blue areas in brain imaging) (Khan 2011). More research is needed to try to understand the relationship between the two but the seamless transition in numerous Treasure Basket observations suggests to me an evolution from exploration to pretend play with exploration often a precursor to imaginative play. A distinction is made between specific exploration, i.e. 'What can this object do?', where the sensorial qualities come to the fore and diversive exploration, where the child focuses on 'What can I do with this object?' (Hutt and Bhavanini 1972, cited in Bruner 1976; Gatch 1976, cited in Oates 1979). Both these behaviours are apparent in Treasure Basket play, contrasting with most conventional toys where the emphasis can remain 'What can this toy do?' (Hughes 2003). Whatever your viewpoint, we have seen how Treasure Basket play generally, and the Continuum in particular, offer countless opportunities for children to familiarize themselves with objects, refine their thinking and practise the 'What can I do?' element of play.

In this chapter we have seen the Continuum in action, gaining a deeper insight into its potential application and benefits to children and practitioners. Offering a Treasure Basket to children older than 12 months of age is clearly a departure from Goldschmied's roots, but there is no mistaking the very special appeal and relevance of this resource and this approach to play for children across the ages. Our attention now turns to the thorny issue of the curriculum and the role of Treasure Baskets, and an understanding of the importance of sensory play generally, in creating an enriching and enabling learning environment.

7 Bringing the curriculum alive

Education is . . . something a child acquires for himself, travelling under his own steam, planning and carrying through each activity as the necessity arises, selecting and using the material at hand for his requirements, adapting himself with intelligence to the needs of every situation and experiencing thereby the happy satisfaction of a completed act.

(Anderson *et al.*, *Activity Methods for Children Under Eight*)

Overview

This chapter introduces the latest phase in the evolution of the UK Early Years curriculum, making the links with sensory-rich Treasure Basket play. The prime and specific areas of the Early Years Foundation Stage (EYFS) (March 2012) will be explored and play observations used to signpost commonalities. It is recognized that this is but one curriculum and that emphasis can and does change. Rather than slavishly following curriculum silos, the remainder of the chapter uses play observations as a tool for highlighting cross-curricular learning, thereby increasing global relevance.

Sensory play and the curriculum

The Statutory Framework for the Early Years Foundation Stage, due to be implemented in September 2012, identifies three prime areas of Personal, social and emotional development; Communication and language; and Physical development, recognizing their crucial role as linchpins in the development of 'well-rounded' children able to access life's opportunities. 'Practitioners working with the youngest children are expected to focus strongly on the three prime areas' (DFE 2012:6). Literacy (L), Mathematics

(M), Understanding the World (UW) and Expressive Arts and Design (EAD) form four specific areas of learning and development. For older children (3 to 5 years) the balance will shift towards 'a more equal focus on all (DFE 2012:6) areas of learning'. While I personally lament the greater emphasis upon 'teaching', 'school readiness' and educational programmes', the narrowing of focus of curriculum areas and lack of value attached to the early years *per se*, the framework does acknowledge the different ways in which children learn, with effective teaching and learning characterized by:

- playing and exploring;
- active learning; and
- creating and thinking critically.

All three of these have a strong synergy with sensory play, a strength which I feel practitioners will need to harness if they are to offset some of the top-down emphasis and potential loss in playfulness of the UK Early Years Curriculum.

A key challenge can be justifying to parents the value of children's play, especially messy play. The Statutory Framework for the EYFS (DFE 2012) attaches great importance to the effective and meaningful engagement of parents, recognizing that this is critical to the life opportunities of future generations. As the following snapshots reveal, deeply absorbing play provides real curricular outputs without the need for expensive or specialist equipment. As such, sensory-rich play is a perfect vehicle for engaging parents in quality play and interactions with their children and fostering an understanding of the benefits of play. The best learning is relevant, real and rooted in children's interests and existing knowledge. This definitely doesn't involve treating different aspects of the curriculum in isolation, but it is helpful to consider how sensory play can contribute to each of the prime areas, specific areas of learning and development and early learning goals (relevant goals identified in bold).

The three prime areas of the Statutory Framework EYFS

1 Personal, social and emotional development (PSED)

Self-confidence and self-awareness

Sand, mud, water, natural resources and a whole raft of other objects typically found in a Treasure Basket or loose parts play are perfect for fostering **self-confidence and self-awareness.** This is true of children across the ages as the resources are open-ended with no right or wrong ways of playing, making them very inclusive and empowering, particularly for children with SEN.

Watch a child deeply engrossed in play and we gain an insight into their personality, interest and schemas (repeated patterns of behaviour). Sustained focus can be indicative of children's contented exploration, problem solving and testing of ideas and theories, common occurrences in sensory play. Take this example of focused exploration and play with a 2-year-old girl. She has just woken up and is sitting next to the Treasure Basket. We join the observation after she has begun play.

> . . . D picks up a tin bucket in her left hand and then uses her right hand to pick up another metal cup. She places it on the top of the tin bucket. D then fiddles with the metal cup while she watches a friend play. She picks up a pine cone and puts it into the metal cup, still watching her friend. D is twisting the pine cone around with her left hand. D then tips the pine cone out as she spots another one on the ground. She leans over sideways to get the pine cone and then places it in a wire egg cup. D then shakes the egg cup until the pine cone falls out. D puts a pine cone in a metal cup and then uses her right hand to poke a piece of ribbon into the different sections of the pine cone. Once the ribbon stays attached to the pine cone [they are both attached to the top of the bucket] she twists them around many times, pulling them taut each time she has twisted them around.

There is something deeply satisfying about setting oneself a challenge and completing it and this is as true of children as it is of adults. In many instances the adult watching will be unaware of the challenge the child has set, but numerous characteristics of deeply focused play and engagement will be apparent. Without branded toys which artificially restrict play, children of markedly different ages (or developmental levels) can happily play side by side, each playing and exploring in a different, yet age-appropriate way. Sadly, the prevalence of mixed-age play is on the decline (Papatheodorou 2010: 18), making opportunities like these all the more important:

> An 8-month-old baby is playing with her Treasure Basket. She has the round woven coaster in her hand, the knitted ball at her foot and a pottery 'pebble' in her other hand held up to her mouth. An 8-year-old enters the room, looks down at the Treasure Basket then crouches down next to it. She sits down and starts taking things out of the basket. After five minutes of looking at the different objects, she begins playing with the wooden spoon and says, 'I'm cooking.' She pauses: 'In fact, I am baking a cake. Could you pass me the eggs.' She looks at the baby and says, 'The eggs.' The baby passes her a woollen ball and the pebble. The 8-year-old then stops when she spots the plug at the bottom of the basket. She starts emptying out the

basket carefully, looking at each object as she does so. She starts to lay these out on the floor, pausing before positioning objects. Meanwhile the baby is contentedly exploring the coaster. The 8-year-old announces that she has designed an obstacle course. She dangles the plug by its chain and hovers it over the objects. She hands me the woollen teddy and says, 'He has to get through the course without contacting the plug and I will time it.' Then she says, 'Wait!' She busily changes all the objects around and starts collecting all the circular objects and puts them down at varying distances from the wooden spoon, teaspoon and big metal spoon. She says, 'Right, gather everyone around. I have a game to play. We have to try and get things into the targets.' She places bits of paper on which she has written numbers on each target; the smallest circle is labelled 25 points and the biggest circle is labelled 5 points. 'I have drawn a table; the smallest one is hardest and that's why you get more points if you get it.'

The 8-year-old plays for two hours, asking to play with the basket again later that day. Throughout the 'session' her play evolves, in line with her thinking perhaps, as she familiarizes herself with the objects, and this opens up their potential to be used in more creative ways. As we shall discover later in this chapter, play with objects can also give rise to wonderful moments of peer mentoring, where a peer helps extend another child's learning, as occurred when three 4-year-olds played with a Treasure Basket and sand in the garden, and a combination of the resources and peer support helped extend a child's learning to the zone of proximal development.

Managing feelings and behaviour
Sensory-rich play can contribute to children's emotional well-being and understanding of themselves and what they can do. If used appropriately this is especially relevant for children with sensory perception difficulties, but also has an important role to be played generally. In one pre-school the Treasure Basket was used as a tool for supporting a child with separation anxiety. Practitioners were at a loss to know how best to support this child, who was inconsolable when her mother left and miserable and detached for the remainder of the session. After this pattern of behaviour continued for two weeks, the key person placed a Treasure Basket on a low table near the door and, with the girl in her arms, said goodbye to the mother as she reached for the basket to show her. Without any tears the child stood at the table and explored the objects, with her key person sitting beside her. (The rest of her peers were in another part of the room for the usual morning introductory-type activities.) Watching the child smiling beatifically as she explored the basket it was hard to believe that she would 'typically' be sad and withdrawn. The objects seemed to act as a bond between the practitioner and child, with

the child yo-yoing between solitary play and sharing an object with the adult. When the other children's session finished there was a sudden rush as they gathered around the basket to play with the objects. This seemed to be accepted by the girl, now sharing both the adult and objects, and her play evolved from single-item exploration to multiple-item play and domestic role-play emulating her peers. Other practitioners have experienced similar success with other 'no expectation' types of resources such as play dough, water or sand, with clear implications for creating and structuring enabling environments (Bilton 2010).

Making relationships

We saw in Chapter 3 how possession of objects is a key factor in children's evolving social relations as well as being crucial to the development of highly social play and complex play themes (Broadhead 2004). The following snapshot of two girls playing with a Treasure Basket at an Activity Centre reveals the delicate balance at play.

> I (aged two- and-a-half years) stops, takes the lid off a small cylindrical tin and puts it to her mouth as if to smell. She spots the miniature flower pot in the basket and exclaims as a smile spreads accross her face. She picks up the pastry brush and dips the bristle end into the flower pot and pretends to 'feed' her older friend (E, aged 4). She holds the pot in one hand and her friend takes the brush from her, using it to stroke I's face. She shows no emotion when the brush is taken. She picks up a foot-shaped nail brush and feels the bristles, then presses it on the floor so the bristles bend. Her friend takes the brush and again she displays no reaction.

2 Communication and language (CL)

In recent years a combination of the education system and a fixation with speaking, reading and writing have resulted in an overemphasis on these milestones. The English language is one of the most complex languages in the world for babies to decode and children to grasp and yet children in the UK are starting school (or school-based work) ever earlier. Sadly, so-called failings in literacy standards are met with more initiatives and increasingly earlier formalized learning, rather than adopting the approach of much of the Westernized world, of recognizing that our children are simply not ready for formalized learning and that play *per se*, not necessarily 'purposeful and planned play' (DFE 2011: 14), provides a firm foundation for life. Not only is there a disconnect between children's innate drive to learn and discover through exploration and play and the world of formalized learning but, as we saw from our tour of the senses and focus on brain development in Chapters 2 and 3, it is apparent that children's bodies are ill-prepared for this emphasis too.

Understanding and encouraging speaking

> Children build up a mental picture of the things around them based on their sensory contact with their environment and the objects in it. They do this when they hold, feel, suck, listen to, look at, shake and throw things.
>
> (Beaver *et al.* 1997: 52)

Although the downplaying of literacy in the *Statutory Framework for the Early Years Foundation Stage* (DFE 2011) is welcomed, the framework itself has a strong emphasis upon speaking and listening and no mention of body language, the mainstay of communication for all of us, let alone infants. We have discovered the role of gestures, cues and body language in helping infants interpret their labelless world as well as providing a means for their pre-verbal communication, and thus it is communication, in its widest sense, which is referred to in this book. The Tickell Review recognized that

> Not enough credibility is given to how important it is for children to play and explore in order for them to develop communication, speaking and listening and social and emotional skills.
>
> (Tickell 2011: 20)

The open-ended nature of most sensory-rich object play is great for enhancing understanding and a necessary precursor to reading and writing. Exploration gives meaning to a whole host of words like soft and hard, hot and cold, heavy and light, rough and smooth, big and small, and their mastery unlocks a sophisticated world of rules, categories and concepts.

> Babies and young children are very sensual beings, touching, tasting, smelling, hearing, exploring the environment and objects visually, using sounds to communicate needs, feelings and ideas long before they have the spoken language of their culture. Babies rely totally on their senses to begin to tell them about the world around them. It is through their senses that babies move towards understanding about the world and begin to construct information and ideas from those sensory play experiences.
>
> (Forbes 2004: 49)

Without actually experiencing these concepts a child cannot meaningfully put a name to them or store memories of them efficiently for future access. As we discovered in Chapter 6, children respond to these resources in very different ways, for example babies and young children may babble as they play and explore, appearing to commentate on their play. Although primarily a 'non-social' activity, the play of babies and young children can have the appearance of a conversation, like the babies described in Chapter 4. Frequently the 'communication' would not have taken place without the objects. Others play in silence, possibly because they are focusing so intently, which is great preparation for **listening and attention**. Unlike many playthings, the unusual open-ended objects that make up a Treasure Basket and element of surprise about what they can do inspires language and critical thinking.

3 Physical development (PD)

Play with highly malleable, open-ended resources is great for developing fine and gross motor skills as well as building strength, key aspects of **moving and handling**. Even very young babies sit absorbed while playing with a Treasure Basket, developing as they do so back, shoulder and arm muscles, as well as building strength. With every movement, hand and finger control improves, as does hand–eye co-ordination, hardwiring children's brains for learning. Milestones like hand–eye co-ordination are the culmination of an interplay between two distinct sensory channels, that of vision and touch. Only when infants have gained sufficient visual control to be able to focus with binocular vision can they confidently master purposeful hand and finger movements necessary for using their hands as tools for extending learning. Unlike adults, children's play is often full-bodied, as is their learning. Consider the challenge of mark-making in dry or wet sand, gloop or mud; splashing in muddy puddles or stretching to climb a tree; squeezing sand or mud between fingers; or painting with a fat brush. All these actions require wide-ranging physical skills and mastery, but these are rarely the goal because they are enriching and fun.

Specific areas of the revised EYFS

Literacy (L)

Physically speaking, by manipulating objects, repeating fine motor skills and using objects as 'tools', children develop the muscle strength and control to achieve the milestone of **writing**. However, as several play vignettes have shown, sensory-rich play resources also have a key role to play in developing reading and mark-making. Open-ended objects and environments inspire spontaneous and meaningful writing and mark-making, like the children who created their own bottling 'business' and developed perfume labels for their bottled concoctions, inspired only by some old-fashioned glass bottles that they'd discovered. Their motive wasn't driven by the curriculum but born out of its relevance to their play theme. **Reading**, writing and speaking, not to mention creativity and problem solving, were welcome by-products of deeply engaged play, both inspired and fuelled by objects.

Mathematics (M)

Set within its wider context, mathematics is in essence problem solving, something which as we have seen in Chapter 3 lies at the heart of young children's genetic make-up and survival in literally trying to make sense of the world. Like the introductory quote, problem solving emerges in countless sensory-rich play experiences, giving meaning to mathematics and science as well as providing rich fodder for language and communication. Janet Moyles identifies numerous instances where the 'preliminaries of being able to understand and solve problems will be encountered' (1989: 63), all of which can be offered through the open-ended objects, resources and opportunities associated with the Sensory Play Continuum. Understanding objects and properties can be exciting, challenging and all-absorbing, giving children agency over their own learning. Due in large part to the open-endedness of sensory play materials, their behaviour and properties throw up numerous opportunities for disequilibrium, surprise, and the investigation of cause and effect, trial and error, pattern, volume and so much more. Water or sand play can help bring **numbers** to life with hands-on challenges like 'how many small pots of water are needed to fill a large pot?' Or 'how many pots of water do you need to sink the paper boat?' Practical, hands-on approaches are essential for children, providing deeply satisfying experiences as well as making **shape, space and measures** relevant and fun. With most of this play child initiated, children show amazing concentration as they focus on the challenge they have presumably set themself: be it how to create a car from loose parts; how to get a long heavy dog chain into a small pot; or how to fit packing peanuts into a tin.

Typical 2- to- 3-year-olds can be seen building towers from objects, matching lids to pans and inserting objects into larger containers. 'The ability to solve such problems provides a window into children's developing spatial perception, mechanical reasoning and goal-directed action' (Shutts *et al.* 2009: 1612), conferring far greater importance to the process than the act itself may suggest. Fox observed 4- and 5-year-old children playing outside and 'found examples of addition and subtraction, shape identification, patterning, one-to-one correspondence, number sense, sequencing of events, use of ordinal numbers, knowledge of prepositions, and identification of final and initial consonants'. Furthermore, numerous 'examples of problem-solving, creative thinking, social competence, language use, and gross and

Figure 7.1 Problem solving in action

fine motor skills' were observed (Fox 1993, cited by Fox 2011: 3). Since a Treasure Basket shares much of the outdoor environment's affordance it is no surprise to find similar skills at large in Treasure Basket play.

Understanding the world (UW)

Sand, mud, water, natural resources and the outdoor environment are great for introducing the characteristics of materials, prompting questions like 'what is this?', 'what is it made of?', 'where does it come from?' and 'what is it used for?' Through play with a Treasure Basket children come to understand the changing properties of resources; master the use of tools – essential for writing later; and enter a world of hands-on scientific discovery. Depending upon the objects they can also introduce **people and communities** and **the world** in a hands-on, inspirational way. **Technology**, too, can be seamlessly linked to sensory-rich play, with stimulating resources inspiring investigation and meaningful use.

Expressive arts and design (EAD)

Sensory-rich play resources like sand, seed pods and stones cry out to be explored in imaginative ways. The lack of a right or wrong way of **exploring and using media and materials** like these makes them perfect for encouraging creativity. In a world where so many toys have limited ways of being used, open-ended resources can inspire music making, art, games and role-play, as numerous play sessions have shown. But this is to underplay their creative potential. As White explains, 'materials that can be transformed by combining or mixing make for especially fascinating and productive play. When materials can be collected, handled, manipulated and moved around, their play value is further enhanced, allowing children to mould and create their play environment' (White 2011: 52), if they are given the time, space and 'permission' to do so. It is my belief that developing children's creativity and imagination should be central goals of the education system. Given children's natural propensity to innovate and create imaginative uses for the simplest of objects, our focus perhaps should be on stopping the educational system and ourselves from crushing this. We have seen how adults' actions can inadvertently limit outcomes; when it comes to encouraging creativity and imagination simple objects and resources that can be shaped by a child's hands or mind win hands down. Take these examples of children **being imaginative** with a miniature terracotta flowerpot:

> An 11-month-old baby places the flowerpot by her doll's mouth and makes a slurping noise. She then picks up her own beaker and drinks from it. [The slurping sound is the same sound her mother made to encourage her to drink.]
>
> A 14-month-old baby holds the mini-flowerpot, babbling as she pushes the pot around her fingers. She looks up. She then stops, turns the pot upside down and stops babbling. She lifts it up and puts it in to her mouth. She touches the hole with her tongue and again the babbling begins but turns into laughter as she brings the flowerpot down in her hand. She shrieks with laughter and smiles as she puts her finger in the hole. She then gets up with the pot still on her finger and walks around showing each adult in the room. She is babbling as she comes over. Her eyes are looking down at her finger. She takes the pot off her finger and slides it across the floor and then looks around at other surfaces, which she touches with the flowerpot. As she does so she looks up then makes a louder noise with the pot which gains people's attention.

A 3-year-old puts the mini-flowerpot on the back of a toy truck. He collects sweet wrappers and puts them in the pot. He puts the flowerpot on the side and tips the wrappers into the truck and moves the truck along. He then comes back to the pot and shouts, 'We need your bins', 'It's bin day!' and looks round at me saying, 'I have to put it all in piles.'

Activity 18

- Ideally playing in teams, try to come up with as many different uses as possible for simple objects like a pastry brush, rubber plug, napkin ring, and so on. These can be fun, unusual, silly or serious ideas but the aim is to try to think of as many uses as possible. If playing as an individual, aim for 20 or more ideas.
- Talk or think about the number and range of ideas for each object and whether this surprises you. Does this cast a new light on the potential value of a Treasure Basket?
- If you're naturally playful and this comes easily, can you use this playfulness to appraise existing provision? For those who find this harder, think about what might help you see simple objects like these with child-like eyes?

Imaginative play should not be restricted to young children or marginalized to free time 'when the work has been done', but valued in its own right for its vital contribution to developing rich and rounded children and adults. The challenge for practitioners is making time and space for the development of such key life skills within the constraints of a curriculum and emphasis upon 'school readiness'.

Broad-based learning

Areas of learning should not take place in isolation but in a seamless and interlinked way. The following snapshots of play provide some examples of this in action, drawing together the key threads of thinking in this chapter.

Context
C (aged 4 years and 6 months), E (aged 4 years and 7 months) and L (aged 4 years and 9 months) are in the small garden in a Children's Centre with the sandpit and Treasure Basket for them to access. This is the second time L has played with this particular basket but she has two new friends to explore with.

Observation

At first the children look only at the basket items, pulling them out one by one, exploring them, discussing them together . . . E picks up a whisk and says, 'I got a big one of these at home; it's for mixing.' L picks up a brush – 'It's a cleaner' and she brushes the sand with it. 'Look, it's making lines in the sand.' E takes over the use of the brush. Carer asks, 'What are you doing with the brush E?' 'I'm getting all the lumps out of the sand' says E, quite out of breath – she is putting in a lot of effort brushing the sand. The three children share and talk about the items. C fills up a pot using the large metal spoon. He turns it over: 'Look, I made a sandcastle', banging the bottom to ensure it comes out. 'Ta- da' he announces proudly. 'Very good C', he says.

E and L find the terracotta pot in the purse. 'Look, ah it's a baby flowerpot', says L. 'It's small, look these ones are bigger', says E, comparing it to the flowerpots in the garden. E fills up the terracotta pot and runs off around the grass area. She runs back to the sandpit and finds the sand is gone. 'Hey. How that happen?' says E. 'My sand all gone!' 'It's got a hole in it E, that's why', says L. Each of the children fill up the pot and run around the garden. When they get back to the sandpit they look to see who has the most sand left.

C picks up the wire metal egg cup and fills it up with sand. He lifts it up and the sand falls out. 'Oh man, it's coming out!' So E says, 'You need some water.' C gets some water and mixes it into the sand, and then puts the sand into the egg cup and says, 'It's staying there.'

Learning points

- This trio of children display excellent communication and thinking skills (CL). They make the links between big and little and are easily able to convey their ideas (M and CL). They develop a game combining creativity with physical development (PD and EAD). They explore the properties of materials and science of cause, effect and change (UW and M). They play with focus, appear confident in their own abilities and understanding and are adept at peer mentoring (PSED). A combination of the open-ended resources and other children at play appear to support learning in the zone of proximal development.
- This session also conveys the key role of the adult in allowing children to make these discoveries for themselves. So easily an adult could have stepped in and solved the issue of the hole, but given the space, time and opportunity to freely explore issues like these, children can discover the answers and adults learn just how much children understand.

The following observation reveals how learning can take place anywhere, even on a busy exhibition stand. Sessions like this emphasize the importance of giving children time and space to solve their own challenges through trial and error. It also highlights the potential value of mess and how, in the concept of 'possibility thinking' children need to find a problem before they can try to solve it (Grainger *et al.* 2007).

Context
Boy aged 3 years plays with a Treasure Basket on a busy education exhibition stand, with his mother sitting nearby.

Observation

> Child F plays happily with a Treasure Basket for about 30 minutes before he notices a drawer in a cupboard beside him containing dried rice. He rummages through the basket and proceeds to use a large metal spoon to fill a miniature flowerpot with dried rice. After refilling the pot numerous times he appears to notice the red carpet, which is now covered with white rice. He tilts the pot, still in his hand, and spots the hole in the bottom of the pot. He starts rummaging through the basket and picks up the pastry brush, which he uses to brush the floor. The rice pings in all directions and is discarded by the boy. He continues rummaging in the basket then picks up the nail brush. He tries stroking this across the carpet and a smile spreads across his face as the short bristles move the rice. As he arcs the brush through the rice he creates red striped patterns on the floor. Apparently distracted from clearing up he notices the patterns he has created and moves the brush, creating more. After some time he resumes tidying the rice up using the brush to sweep the rice into the large metal spoon and transferring it to a measuring cup with handle to return it to the drawer of rice, still in the cupboard. [The boy continued until all the rice had been cleared away, with no help or prompts.]

Learning points

- In this child-led session the child explored problem solving and trial and error. He appeared to pursue his own goals of getting the rice out of the drawer, filling the pot, making patterns and clearing up the rice (PSED, M, PD, EAD). He demonstrated great focus and concentration and did not appear to be fazed by the 'messy problem' that he'd created (PSED). He showed great creativity through the approach he applied to 'the challenge' and in the patterns that he created (EAD). He showed a good understanding and use of tools and great fine and gross motor skills, hand–eye co-ordination and manipulation (UW, EAD and PD). No verbal communication was used, but his body language appeared to convey to both adults present that he was happy and 'in control' (PSED and CL).

- As importantly, his mother allowed him to make a mess and solve the problem himself, neither rescuing nor rebuking him, but respecting and watching his play instead.

Activity 19

Observe one or more children playing with open-ended resources like a Treasure Basket, sand or water, heuristic play or loose parts play. Simply watch what they do, how they play, what objects they use, and any language used. Record any areas where you feel you could support the children in extending their learning (on another occasion). List any surprises or learning points. How will this affect what you do or offer in the future?

Curriculum-led learning

Chapter 9 explores the part adults play in offering enabling environments for play and exploration. If we get this right, opportunities for achieving curriculum outputs naturally unfold. If, however, the curriculum is the starting point, lacklustre sessions like these can emerge.

> The practitioner asks E to find a big bucket and she successfully finds the big sand bucket. She's then asked to find the little bucket. E correctly finds the miniature silver bucket from the Treasure Basket. E then correctly points and says, 'Big bucket', 'Little bucket.' She correctly says the colour of the two buckets: 'blue' and 'grey'.

Compare this to the immediacy, relevance and vividness of the three 4-year-olds exploring volume, size and properties with sand outside, and it is clear how the bucket session lacks richness and vibrancy.

One of the things I most love about watching play with a Treasure Basket is the element of the unexpected. Far from pigeonholing play, numerous examples of divergent thinking can be seen from children using brushes and pots to paint with; creating an oven from a chain; creating people with some or all of the objects; making up games and stories; or using loofahs as weapons of intergalactic combat! Hands-on, open-ended resources like these can tap into children's imagination and fuel their innate drive to learn, delivering real curriculum outputs in the process. Before considering the key role of the adult in facilitating this, we now turn to the particular challenges faced by children with sensory processing difficulties, who need a helping hand in reaping the rich rewards of play.

8 Sensory processing and special educational needs

The sensory piece for many children has been overlooked, downplayed, or undervalued for too long. Now is the time to bring sensory dysfunction into the forefront and begin to look at home and school learning and behaviour differently – through a sensory lens.

(Emmons and Anderson, *Understanding Sensory Dysfunction*)

Overview

With 'over 80 per cent of the nervous system involved in processing or organizing sensory input' (Ayres 2005) and all learning in the brain ultimately stemming from sensory stimulation, the importance of our senses and providing ample and appropriate opportunities for stimulation are apparent. In Chapter 2 we explored the external and internal senses as they are typically experienced. However, for some children with special educational needs (SEN), sensory stimulation can present itself in unusual ways, which in turn affects their knowledge and interpretation of the world. A learning environment rich in sensory experiences can benefit everyone provided we have a good understanding of children's individual sensory needs, including which stimuli to avoid. If we get it wrong, children's lives are at best a constant challenge and at worst a source of discomfort and pain, which is why this chapter focuses exclusively on SEN, an area where one size does not fit all. With no two children the same, it is not possible to explore sensory stimulation and SEN in fine detail, but this chapter flags up some sensory challenges and implications, and in doing so will hopefully increase knowledge and understanding of this largely hidden problem.

Sensory processing disorder is 'characterized by a range of atypical behavioural responses to ordinary sensory stimulation' (Miller *et al.* 2009: 1). Within this spectrum, sensory over-responsivity, sensory under-responsivity and sensory seeking problems may be apparent. Typical over-responsivity behaviours include feeling overwhelmed by sensory inputs and showing 'fight or flight' and defensive responses to one or more types of sensory stimuli, that would not be overwhelming for neuro-typically developed children. Far from being a rare phenomenon, research suggests that 5 to 16 per cent of school age children have negative responses to sensory stimuli affecting their participation in everyday life (Brett-Green *et al.* 2010). It is also believed that sensory processing problems may lie missed or masked behind diagnoses of autism, autistic spectrum disorders (ASD) and other learning difficulties. As we discovered in Chapter 2, all human learning stems from the sensory information that the body and brain derives from the environment. As evidenced on our tour of the senses, a problem with any one sense impacts upon another and 'interactions among the senses profoundly influence behaviour, perception, emotion and cognition' (Miller *et al.* 2009: 6). Goddard (1996: 41) identifies three elements to the system which need to be in place for this to operate efficiently:

1   The reception of information via the senses.
2   The processing of information in the brain.
3   Information passing from the brain to the body.

I will now consider each of these in turn with a view to identifying potential problem areas.

1 The reception of information via the senses

In Chapter 2 we discovered the complex mechanisms in place for capturing sensory information. For most of us this system works efficiently, providing and processing information with accuracy and no apparent effort on our part. Take the example of listening, an incredibly complex process involving both hearing and the processing of sounds. Sound also has several dimensions: loudness, frequency or pitch, duration and localization, i.e. where the sound comes from (Biel and Peske 2009: 40). A child with sensory processing problems may struggle to put together all these different elements to provide a coherent 'picture' or experience difficulty in one of these dimensions, such as sounds being too loud or too quiet, discomfort from particular frequencies, or too much 'white noise'. With sight, hypersensitivity to light or problems discerning detail from backgrounds may impact upon a child's ability to see. Alternatively a child's vision may be otherwise perfect but if the ocular muscles don't work together to provide binocular vision, then a child will have difficulty in engaging in everyday activities like reading, writing or walking. The sense of taste and smell are inextricably linked to give most of us great pleasure and satisfaction but for children unable to 'tune out', or hypersensitive to smells, this can affect concentration, eating behaviour, and everyday actions like brushing teeth or going to school.

The role of reflexes

Babies are born with a series of primitive reflexes, designed to prepare them for the best possible start in life. The Moro reflex manifests as a 'startle' response when sudden sound, movement, light, pain or temperature change are encountered. Typically this disappears at 2 to 4 months of age, otherwise a child will remain in a heightened state of awareness (Goddard 1996: 6), over-reacting to sudden stimuli and producing stress hormones which set in place a vicious cycle of sensitivity and response. 'The child who still has a Moro reflex will experience the world as too full of bright, loud and abrasive sensory stimuli' and therefore be overloaded with sensory information which merges as one (Goddard 1996: 6). The palmar reflex manifests as a light touch to the palm resulting in a baby's fingers closing. Evident in some mammals when 'flexing' their hands while feeding (Goddard 1996: 8), this reflex demonstrates the fundamental link between the hands and mouth. Play with a Treasure Basket provides a great example of this in action, as young babies will inevitably mouth any object that they grasp. It also corresponds with the higher incidence of sensory receptors in these areas. By 4–6 months this reflex should be inhibited as a pincer grip develops, followed by the ability to release an object, a key milestone in Treasure Basket play. Failure to inhibit this reflex will impact upon a child's ability to explore his or her environment and master fine motor skills like writing.

Evident at birth, the tonic labyrinthine reflex manifests as forward and backward movements of the head. The continued presence of this reflex will affect children's ability to crawl and walk, as they will struggle to judge space, distance and speed (Goddard 1996: 17) and acquire the necessary balance. 'It is through crawling and creeping that the raw materials of seeing, feeling and moving synchronize for the first time to provide a more complete picture of the environment' (Goddard 1996: 18). The close links between movement and visual acuity are further supported by research into the Xinguana Indians in South America, who have amazing distance vision but are unable to focus on anything closer than arm's length. The reason for this is believed to stem from babies being carried on their mother's backs as the environment is not safe for crawling (Vera 1975, cited in Goddard 1996: 21). Problems with any of the primitive reflexes described can help account for sensory information reception and processing difficulties.

2 Processing information in the brain

As we discovered in Chapter 2, our miraculous brain is the processing centre for sensory information. One of its most important roles is 'regulating sensory input so that the level of alertness is proportional to the intensity of sensory stimulation a person experiences' (Biel and Peske 2009: 20). With the brain constantly bombarded with sensory information, much of which is irrelevant, the brain achieves this through a neurological process called inhibition, whereby unimportant sensory messages are filtered out – such as the sensation of wearing clothes. This works in tandem with the process of facilitation, whereby attention is drawn to the important sensory messages received. If operating in harmony, a child can self-regulate to achieve a balance but for children with sensory processing difficulties, balance and control are elusive qualities. In addition to the mechanisms controlling the amount of sensory information received, the cerebellum is believed to operate like a 'volume control knob', regulating the intensity of sensory input (Biel and Peske 2009: 65). A problem with this results in too intense a sensory input (be it sound, touch, movement, taste or vision) being received by an individual, with concomitant problems of over-stimulation. As children learn through their senses, difficulty in interpreting, integrating and using sensory information from their internal and external senses may affect their development and understanding generally. 'Like constructing a building on sand, if you don't have a firm foundation of reliable sensory information, you lack a solid base on which to build all those developmental skills' (Biel and Peske 2009: 5).

3 Information passing from the brain to the body

All sensory input, other than olfactory, travels through the hypothalamus, which relays it to the appropriate part of the body. If this 'sensory switchboard' is faulty this will impact upon the process by which sensory information is enacted, which brings us to the final stage of processing. Typically, when a child learns something, the information from the sensory environment travels through the central nervous system to the brain to be analysed. A message is sent to the appropriate part of the body and an action results, such as 'let go', if holding a hot pan. If operating efficiently, a cycle develops between the sensory stimulus, mind and body, with feedback from each stage forming a fundamental part of the learning process (Macintyre 2010).

Key sensory problems

For many people with SEN, sensory processing difficulties manifest themselves as a number of key challenges, as follows.

Lack of feedback and habituation

A lack of feedback can make it difficult for some children with SEN to learn from situations, so they repeat the same mistakes or need to relearn every movement as though for the first time. Most of us take this for granted when learning complex actions like riding a bike or learning to write as, once mastered, these actions are consigned to our subconscious. Evidence suggests that children who overreact to sensory experiences don't habituate but instead feel the experience over and over again as though for the first time.

Activity 20

- Imagine how difficult daily functions might be and how much time it would take if you had to relearn everything as new. What effect might this have on your confidence, ability to do something quickly, or focus?
- Imagine you are sitting on a beanbag listening to a story. Now imagine being bombarded with constant irrelevant sensory information like 'I can feel the beanbag that I'm sitting on moving.' How might this affect your ability to focus or function in everyday life?

Over- and under-stimulation

Children with SEN, and particularly autism, are often more sensitive to sensory stimulation, experiencing either over- (hyper)sensitivity or under- (hypo)sensitivity to stimuli. This can relate to any of the senses, with hyperstimulation expressed as constant interference even leading to actual pain from noise, light, touch, taste, and so on, and hyposensitivity a need for sensory stimulation to satisfy a lack of sensory feedback. In some children, hypersensitivity can mean they are painfully sensitive to touch and need a lot of personal space. In others the trigger may be noise, smells or taste, or a combination of these as this condition is rarely confined to a single sense. An example of this is some people's repulsion at the 'smell of being touched', something generally inconceivable. Many children can experience hypersensitivity for one sense and hyposensitivity for another, or the degree of sensitivity and whether it is hyper or hypo can change on a daily basis, making it difficult to plan for their needs.

Activity 21

Imagine what it might be like to be hypersensitive to particular sensory stimuli.

- Do any of the children in your care display signs of over- or under-sensitivity?
- Liaise closely with parents and observe carefully (particularly behaviour labelled as 'naughty') to see if you can gain a better picture of a child's sensory world.

For young children there is considerable scope for conflict in group situations as some may need (or simply be accustomed to) loud noise, touch or visual stimulation while others are fearful of this for the pain that it causes. Many potential sources of pain, discomfort, fear and distraction may not be obvious to practitioners, as they do not affect them. Examples might be problems caused by a profusion of colours, or the otherwise imperceptible flicker of a fluorescent light; shrill sounds, or simply too many simultaneous sounds; the use of particular, scented cleaning materials; or trying foods with new textures. Within an early years or primary school setting, this can inadvertently disrupt children's involvement and learning as we may be unaware of the potential distractions that they face.

Activity 22

Think about how we can adapt children's play and learning environments to meet the needs of all children better. For example, create private spaces and dens to provide quiet, calm and refuge; restructure the day to give children adequate time to become absorbed in play as well as opportunities to revisit activities and extend learning; offer play opportunities outdoors.

Returning to the Learning Tools introduced in Chapter 3, children with developmental delay may experience particular placing challenges due to a dislike of touching or exploration. Other potential obstacles to play may include an obsession with one object to the detriment of exploring others or limited opportunities for actually picking up and placing because of a child's pace of movement or other disabilities. Any one of these factors can reduce a child's exposure to picking and placing and so limit development.

Lack of sensory gatekeepers

It is now believed that over-responsivity is attributed to sensory information processing occurring within the higher level frontal areas rather than in the lower level cortical regions of the brain and poor inhibition of 'irrelevant' sensory input, with typically developed children displaying more 'gating' of such stimuli. Children with sensory processing difficulties find it difficult to 'tune out' repetitive and irrelevant stimulation, which has profound effects upon quality of life, social interactions and self-esteem. Donna Williams, an acclaimed autistic author, describes 'how her problem in infancy was not so much that she did not understand the world, but that she could not stand it, because she was so often bombarded with an overload of sensory information' (Theo Peeters in Bogdashina 2003: 14).

Focus on detail

With their bodies constantly bombarded by sensory stimuli some children with SEN, particularly those on the autistic spectrum, may tend to focus on particular details rather than 'seeing the bigger picture'. One autistic child likened daily life to an untuned radio. When tuned in he was able to engage in satisfying human interactions, but when fuzzy he would avoid such interactions (Bogdashina 2003: 66).

Activity 23

Turn on the radio and adjust the frequency so that you hear lots of background noise, but not any particular station properly.

- Now imagine that you are in a room and you can hear a chair move or a rubber drop on the floor in another room. How easy would it be for you to concentrate on what somebody is saying to you?
- Imagine that the radio station keeps tuning in and out of focus so that one minute it is crystal clear and the next blurry. How difficult would it be to understand all the instructions for a task or the plot of a story?
- How can we support all children, but particularly those experiencing hyper- or hyposensitivity, to be more included?

Mono channel focus

Many people with SEN may only be able to receive and process information from one sensory source at a time, making it difficult literally to make sense of the world. Turning off one sensory channel to focus on another, known as mono channel, is common in children with autism who have developed this as a coping mechanism. Sparrow (2011) recognized this difficulty in children with cerebral visual impairment as they are unable to parallel process information from more than one sense at a time. To support such a child it is helpful to reduce the multi-sensory dimension of the environment. Offering just a few objects from a Treasure Basket initially can help prepare them for the multi-sensory world.

Lack of integration

In Chapter 2 we explored the senses one by one. While this focus on individual senses is helpful to increase baseline understanding, neuroscientists now realize that such compartmentalization is misleading as 'real world experiences are multi-sensory in nature, and thus studying how the senses interact is essential' (Miller *et al.* 2009: 6). It is also emerging that the human brain (like that of cats) may actually consist of multi-sensory as well as uni-sensory cells, the former being receptive to sound, sight, touch and pressure (Miller *et al.* 2009: 3). In fact much of the brain is now believed to be multi-sensory and not simply those areas where input from different sensory sources converge. Furthermore, it is now thought that the effectiveness of individual senses is 'amplified when combined, conferring greater importance to the multisensory stimuli' (Meredith and Stein 1983, cited in Miller *et al.* 2009: 7). When the senses do not act together as they should, known as 'sensory integration' (Ayres 1972), this results in delays in processing information, with a knock-on effect on comprehension, not to mention confusion about interpreting conflicting sensory information.

Sensory problems and autism spectrum disorders (ASD)

Studies have shown that the nervous system of people with autism responds very differently to sensory input, revealing two distinct patterns of arousal and sensory reactivity, either over-or under-arousal (Biel and Peske 2009; Schoen *et al.* 2008). Tactile defensiveness, where a child is reluctant to touch certain materials, is also common. In fact there is an argument for the Triad of Impairments (Wing 1992) characteristic of ASD being reclassified, with sensory processing difficulties representing a fourth strand or an overarching tier as many aspects of the 'social interaction' and 'communication' strands are inextricably linked to sensory processing difficulties. Given what we've discovered about the need for children to decode the world before they can move on to pretend play, this may also be a limiting factor when it comes to 'imagination', the third 'strand'. Although we have much to learn about the manifestation of sensory processing problems, evidence suggests that these underlie a whole host of learning difficulties.

Positive actions

As children grow they become better at dealing with uncomfortable sensory stimuli, typically adopting three types of coping mechanisms to deal with sensory challenges:

- Tuning out detaches a child from the world's sensory stimuli.
- Antisocial behaviour such as aggression or loudness gives individuals control over their world, or an outlet for pent-up frustration.
- Self-stimulatory behaviours, such as flapping hands or humming, helps block out competing stimuli and communicates frustration or emotional needs.

With all aspects of a child's life affected by sensory problems, Biel and Peske suggest a two-pronged approach to achieving 'a foundation of sensory well-being needed to learn, play, socialise, and live up to their full potential' (2009: 5).

1   Making changes to the physical environment to meet the child's unique needs.
2   Supporting children's own ability to tolerate and integrate sensory information.

This recognizes the importance of making environmental as well as individual-based interventions and the essential role of adults in achieving this. In reality the individual and environment are inextricably linked and perhaps the second of these should be viewed as two complementary areas, distinguishing between tolerating sensory problems and integrating and processing sensory stimuli. Regardless of SEN, many children find paying attention challenging. A number of proactive strategies can help, such as allowing the use of sensory-rich resources to provide sensory feedback; providing quiet spaces to sit in calmly and take time out; minimizing other distractions; and using attractive resources to incentivize less preferred activities (Macintyre 2005: 97). As with all children, it is a case of understanding each individual to discover the types of resources or activities that will best meet their needs. For many children with sensory processing problems communication can be difficult, so self-stimulation behaviours can provide an insight into what they may be experiencing and what support they need. By reflecting upon this, adults can understand possible causes, identify which sensory domains are involved and shape the child's environment to support needs in the best possible way.

The notion of improving sensory processing has emerged in response to our greater awareness of the plasticity of the brain and the possibility for rewiring it to integrate sensory information. A fundamental tenet of Ayres' Sensory Integration Therapy is the coupling of an enriched environment with appropriate stimulation. It is with this in mind that the concept of a 'sensory diet' has emerged, a system for providing sensory input to help calm the child and reorganize their sensory wiring.

A sensory diet

All children, but particularly those with autism, benefit from being in a 'just right' state, where they are neither over- nor under-stimulated. Accessing a 'diet' of appropriate sensory-rich play and learning opportunities at regular intervals throughout the day can help children achieve this (Wilbarger and Wilbarger 1991). Like the diets that we are more commonly familiar with, a combination of 'sensory main meals' and 'sensory snacks' help us stay in a 'just right' state. A sensory room is great for providing a sensory workout or 'main meal' but sensory stimulation also needs to take place between these times, in non-specialized environments, involving little or no specialist planning or provision. 'Sensory snacks' are opportunities for children to play with sensory-rich resources in situ, making them perfect for use in early years settings, mainstream schools and in the home. So what might a sensory-rich learning environment look like in practice?

The sensory room – a sensory 'main meal'

All-encompassing provision like pools and gyms can offer large-scale sensory experiences, albeit at a price and on a scale that may limit provision to specialist schools. A sensory room or temporary den is an all-singing, all-dancing sensory environment with much to offer children with SEN. The coloured lights, dark and calm environment, sounds and sights of bubbles and water can be controlled to make a real difference to children's lives, providing a respite from constant sensory overload. Although multi-sensory by name, the resources can be predominantly plastic or fabric, offering little in the way of sensory stimulation, so this may be something to consider if the children who will be accessing the 'room' benefit from tactile stimulation.

The outdoor environment – a 'main meal' or 'sensory snack'

With a rightful emphasis upon outdoor play opportunities within the early years curriculum, making the case for access to outdoors is not difficult. However, what happens there is key. A distinction between formal learning indoors and 'running around' outdoors is unhelpful, limiting the real play and learning potential of the outdoor environment and marginalizing it as simply a place to 'let off steam'. In Chapter 1 the benefit of the environment to health and well-being was cited, with a study revealing that even five minutes' exposure to green spaces generated positive effects upon children's mood and self-esteem, improved attention and, for children with ADHD, significantly reduced their symptoms. The presence of water in the environment increased this still further, with research suggesting the greener the environment the better (Barton and Pretty 2010). When children with ADHD were taken on a 20-minute walk in the park this revealed similar elevated attention levels to a dose of Ritalin. Furthermore, simply providing views of green areas increased attention and reduced impulsiveness among those without ADHD, particularly girls (Sigman 2011).

The outdoor environment can offer both a 'sensory snack' and 'main meal', avoiding much of the sensory overload so difficult for children with sensory processing problems. The therapeutic benefits were apparent in a research project carried out by a Children's Centre. Six 3- to 4-year-old children with wide-ranging additional needs were taken on weekly visits to a wild space in a local wood. Over a period of nine months the challenge, calm, space, freedom from loud noises and other sensory irritants, as well as the changing environment, were found to have increased children's confidence, communication, cognitive development and attitude to risk.

> The forest environment seemed a wonderful place to stimulate all of the senses in a natural and balanced way. Sensory integration appeared to work very effectively and all children showed that they were able to process whether a sensation was from their own body or from the environment.
>
> (Hill, 2010).

Treasure Baskets – a 'sensory snack'

A Treasure Basket is an example of a sensory-rich and highly portable resource, making it a perfect 'sensory snack'. Within an enabling environment children can investigate objects, experiment, or be guided with activities. The sensory stimulation and hands-on approach is great for brain and memory development, gross and fine motor skills and strength. With no right or wrong ways of playing, they can appeal to children with different learning styles and abilities and provide valuable opportunities for self-regulation. One 11-year-old with SEN started tapping the objects, which sparked a song with his 5-year-old sibling, a joyous and rare moment of equality. For some children a basket full of treasures would be too stimulating, in which case these can be offered individually, or just a few at a time. Other children may need heavy items removed (to avoid potential danger from throwing), more robust alternatives to be provided, or to be supported in moving play on to avoid overly repetitious play.

Treasure Baskets and SEN

Since sensory processing interferes with the ability to interact with people and objects, it seems logical that children with sensory processing difficulties (SPD) may have difficulty playing. Studies reveal that children with ADHD (sharing similar characteristics to SPD) generally play for shorter periods of time, find it difficult to return to an activity if interrupted, move around and play more noisily than typically developed children (Barkley 1996; Leipold and Bundy 2000, both cited in Bundy *et al.* 2007). In one session at a busy Activity Centre a 3-year-old was deeply engaged in play with a Treasure Basket. His carer interrupted him with repeated requests that he come and say goodbye to a friend. Reluctantly he left the basket. On his return to the room he did not resume his seated play but instead picked up the metal tin from the Treasure Basket and blew into it, while standing. He repeated this, making loud noises into the tin (enjoying the noise, feel or vibration perhaps?) as he walked around the room. Some children with multiple learning difficulties may engage in disappointing repetitive or uninspired play with a Treasure Basket, in which case consider introducing a range of low or no cost interventions like those listed in Table 8.1.

Making your Treasure Basket more inclusive

Obviously a good Treasure Basket should include a mix of sensory interest, but its effectiveness may be further enhanced by accentuating a particular sensory domain or fine tuning the environment in which the resource is offered. Here are some ideas for improving children's access to a Treasure Basket in each of the Continuum stages.

Table 8.1 Improving access to a Treasure Basket using the Sensory Play Continuum

Action	Objective/Benefit
Stage 1 – Free play	
Add extra objects that will appeal to a child's sense of smell.	Good for a child with a visual or auditory impairment or a hypo-olfactory child who craves smell stimulation.
Add extra objects that provide visual contrast, e.g. variety of patterns and tonal contrasts.	Great for a child with a visual impairment but who can still make out contrasting colours and pattern.
Offer a Treasure Basket in a den, cosy quiet space, or outside to minimize interruptions and distractions.	Good for calming a child and providing a respite from sensory bombardment.
Offer just a few objects on an individual tray or 'play station' for each child.	For a child hypersensitive to touch or easily distracted by peers this can provide much needed space. For a child in a wheelchair this can facilitate play.
Add specific objects or create personalized Treasure Baskets to appeal to a child's particular interest, e.g. metal objects.	Some children with SEN particularly enjoy metal objects so a collection of metal items could be a good way of getting them involved in Treasure Basket play. (See Chapter 4 for more ideas.)
Position the Treasure Basket on a mat to zone the space, provide comfort and minimize interruptions.	With some carpets highly patterned, a floor mat can provide a neutral backdrop to the Treasure Basket objects, as well as extra comfort to prolong play. A mat can also be used to zone spaces, acting as a virtual barrier for other children.
Follow a set routine to prepare children for play and provide reassurance.	Singing a particular song before playing or at tidy-up time can provide auditory cues. Similarly a set routine for getting the mat and basket out can help prepare children for play. Use 'traffic lights' or an egg timer to prepare children for the session ending.
Add uncharacteristic Treasure Basket objects, e.g. flashing rubber balls, vibrating bugs and other similar sensory 'toys' that you know will appeal.	Use the appeal of sensory-feedback toys to capture a child's attention or to encourage a reluctant child to explore and play.
Stage 2 – Combining with other resources	
Provide objects with handles for children who are tactile defensive to play with in sand.	By using a long-handled object as a tool, children who would not otherwise play with some resources, particularly sand, can be included and may even begin to reduce their tactile defensiveness.

(Continued overleaf)

Table 8.1 Continued

Action	Objective/Benefit
Add bubbles or glitter to water to add sensory appeal.	This can work as a reward for a child playing with a non-preferred resource or an enticement for them to explore.
Hide a child's object of interest, e.g. toy cars in the sand to encourage a reluctant child to play.	Many children with ASD develop special interests and it is difficult to get them interested in anything else. Use a child's special interest as a way of encouraging other play.
Play alongside other peers who may engage in pretend play.	Offering the resources alongside children of mainstream development can help children develop their play in ways that might not otherwise happen, e.g. more complex or pretend play.
Stage 3 – Structured activity	
Pick an activity that builds upon the child's interest and use this as a vehicle for introducing the Treasure Basket for play.	Like special interest objects, if you can find activities that build upon a special interest then they will be keen to play.
Use the objects for simple sensory stimulation activities like 'brushing' the arms and legs.	Firm brushing with a loofah or brush tends to be favoured over soft stroking as this can be an irritant. Avoid if a child is over-sensitive to touch.
Use the structure of activities as a tool for introducing a child to a Treasure Basket for free play.	Having been introduced to the resource via the comforting structure of an activity some children with SEN have subsequently followed peers' lead and explored the objects in free play. This realization led to the development of Stage 3 of the Continuum.
If appropriate, combine music or movement to activities to add to the appeal of this resource.	Only do so if a parent or Occupational Therapist has suggested such an approach. Be careful to avoid sensory overload.

Diagnostic difficulties

The cause of sensory processing difficulties is not conclusive, although numerous theories exist (May-Benson *et al.* 2009; Biel and Peske 2009). Diagnosis is equally problematic, especially given that some coping mechanisms disguise over-stimulation as under-stimulation; 'mixed reactivity' (where tolerance changes) can be misinterpreted as 'difficult' behaviour; and a child's control over the stimuli affects response, e.g. a child enjoying making, but not tolerating, loud noises. An individual's ability to 'override' behaviour can mask problems and delay diagnosis and the compartmentalization of treatment further exacerbates this. With infants a Treasure Basket can be a valuable aid in identifying potential problems. Take this example of four babies under 8 months of age sitting around a Treasure Basket. Three of the four were eager, excited and exploring the objects, while the fourth, a very passive baby, did not take part. She was later diagnosed with severe developmental delay (Stroh *et al.* 2008).

Sensory processing difficulties – the adult's role

Activity 24

In Chapter 9 we will explore the adult's role in encouraging sensory play and supporting children with sensory processing difficulties. In the meantime here are some questions for reflecting upon existing practice. Do you/the setting/home:

- observe children to understand what sort of sensory stimulations they enjoy and those they find difficult?
- base activities on knowledge of sensory likes and dislikes?
- respect children's needs and responses and try to understand what they might be experiencing?
- give clear and simple instructions?
- break activities into simple stages and increase complexity in minute steps, only if and when appropriate to do so?
- assume that you can build upon previous play and learning? (This may never be possible and can be frustrating or lower self-esteem.)
- have high expectations or inadvertently limit outcomes?
- give adequate time for children to think, explore and become accustomed?
- provide appropriate visual or auditory cues, e.g. traffic lights or an egg timer, to prepare children for what is expected, what will happen, when it will happen and when it will stop?
- provide spaces and opportunities for meeting children's different needs, be it through stimulation or quiet and calm?
- know typical developmental milestones so that you can flag up potential problems to raise with healthcare professionals?

This chapter has sought to introduce how sensory processing problems manifest in children with SEN. Since all learning starts with our senses, sensory-rich play should be a natural ingredient in any enabling environment, but for children with SEN understanding the sensory challenges they face is key to giving them the best possible start in life. We will now turn to the adult's crucial role in shaping the sensory environment.

9 Adults – getting the balance right

When children's play culture is taken seriously, the conditions which make it flourish are carefully created. Children's play culture does not just happen naturally. Play needs time and space. It needs mental and material stimulation to be offered in abundance.

(Kalliala, *Play Culture in a Changing World*)

Overview

In Chapter 1 we introduced the interplay between the environment, children's needs and adults in terms of determining the quality of play itself and appraising existing sensory provision. Throughout this book, theoretical and practical content has been augmented by a series of activities aimed at increasing understanding in one or more of these areas. This chapter draws together the observations provided in Chapters 5 and 6 for using the Sensory Play Continuum and our knowledge of children's particular sensory needs, to explore adults' crucial yet evolving role in realizing sensory play opportunities.

Adults have a key role to play in providing safe yet stimulating resources, the space and time to explore these fully and freely, and appropriate support to extend play and learning. This is particularly true of sensory play given its association with mess and its immersive qualities once play is under way. Throughout the book we have discovered how rapidly our understanding of the brain is evolving and yet the links between this and the world of early years education remain largely absent. Without greater co-operation there is a danger that we will fail to fully appreciate children's potential and recognize their sensory needs, essential ingredients for creating a truly nurturing and facilitative environment.

Appraising sensory provision

As we have discovered, opportunities for sensory play lie all around us, often limited only by adults' attitude and imagination. If we take the time to observe **children** playing we gain an understanding of their interests, developmental milestones and existing knowledge, and can better plan for their needs. It also helps us see the simplest of **environments** and resources with fresh eyes, ensuring that **adult** interventions are well-measured and appropriate. Watching an 8-month-old baby deeply engaged in exploring a natural woven coaster for nearly an hour, or a 3-year-old exploring sand with Treasure Basket objects for three hours, pinpoints something wonderful in action and we need to take heed and be sure that we are offering the right ingredients for supporting such quality interactions. The relationship between the environment, child and adult is evident and, as Figure 9.1 shows, also forms the basis of a framework for appraising existing sensory provision.

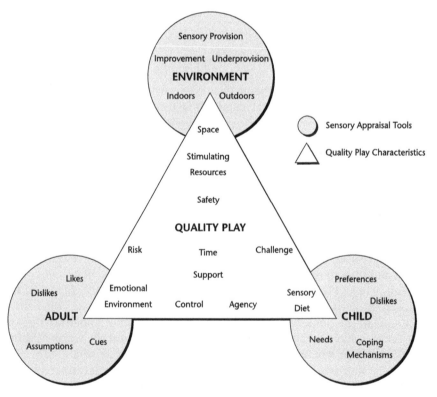

Figure 9.1   The interplay between environment, adult and child

As part of the role of planning how best to meet the sensorial needs of different children it is important to appraise the existing environment, reflect upon children's individual involvement and needs, and assess our own sensory position. We will now consider these three dimensions of sensory provision in turn:

Creating an enabling environment

Questions to consider

- Are any senses particularly well catered for?
- Are any senses currently under-stimulated?
- Could the sensory environment be improved with simple actions? (NB Look at the environment from a child's perspective, which means literally getting down to their level.)

In order to answer these questions we first need to define what constitutes an enabling environment. It is clear that children generally do not need specialized resources or environments in order to enjoy quality play and providing sensory stimulation is not necessarily about 'cranking up all the senses'. When it comes to outdoor spaces, unkempt wild areas offer so much more play potential than manicured lawns and flowerbeds. Adults do, however, have a role in making opportunities such as these available, which in turn requires a recognition of their value for children's play. In order to rise to the challenge of offering an appropriate environment (both physical and emotional) and stimulating resources we first need to define what constitutes stimulating and whose definition will prevail. Most parents (and even some practitioners) will not see the word 'stimulating' emblazoned across the contents of a Treasure Basket, and yet, with such high levels of involvement typical, this would certainly seem to be the case. Stimulating does not necessarily equate with 'all singing all dancing' toys. As the proverbial cardboard box clearly shows, often 'less is more'. Ultimately, care needs to be taken in deciding what is and is not stimulating, as in the hands of an imaginative child that same cardboard box can become a car, castle or spaceship; a collection of objects a tea party or intergalactic weapons; a handful of seedpods a fairy's feast or 'dinosaur poo'! Frequently the only barrier to children enjoying such open-ended resources and environments is our own open-mindedness as adults!

The physical environment

Geraghty suggests that 'materials should be made available in such a way that the child's curiosity leads him to explore, discover various properties of the play equipment, and ask questions about them' (1990: 193). Most natural outdoor environments do this effortlessly. In the UK the importance of play outdoors has become increasingly valued, with access to the outdoor environment a key indicator of quality provision. Although White (2011: 46) rightly urges practitioners to plan provision holistically both indoors and outdoors, this does not necessarily mean that the same resource in different locations provides the same experience. In Norway, sand and water areas are typically located outdoors where, whatever the weather, children access these for digging, exploring and investigation. Educators did not see the need to provide these resources indoors, on a smaller scale, an argument that I have also heard in the UK. However, when practitioners did introduce sand and water play indoors they witnessed benefits for children and changes to their play. Children continued outdoor themes indoors and played more interactively with their peers (perhaps due to the space restrictions). In particular 'the teachers observed that the children's play allowed them to connect emotional expression with physical and imaginative engagement' (Broadhead 2004: 8).

Practitioners were particularly struck by the experience of a 6-year-old Norwegian boy, relatively new to the setting and not particularly integrated within the group. For this little boy the indoor water tray became a catalyst for sharing his anxieties about his father who was away fishing, providing a channel for communication with practitioners and peers. As a result he became better assimilated within the group and practitioners reflected upon their learning and the dangers of making assumptions about provision. As practitioners (and parents) we need to be mindful of examples like this and how they illuminate the impact of both location and scale upon children's play and interactions.

Stimulating resources

A key aspect of the environment in its widest sense is the provision of stimulating resources. We discovered in Chapter 3 that 'versatile, open-ended resources offer an enormous range of possibilities for play, can be used differently by every child and can be naturally transformed into anything the child wants them to be, developing symbolic thinking' (White 2011: 51). This seems to be borne out by the 4-year-old boy (mentioned in Chapter 6) who only engaged in domestic role-play with Treasure Basket objects rather than plastic and wooden play food. 'If the physical environment is over-defined and organized [like the play food perhaps?] it limits the very play it is trying to encourage' (White 2011: 71). An enabling environment should present children with plenty of opportunities for them to follow and develop their interests, but without providing so many resources that children are 'paralysed' with indecision. Research revealed that the majority of adults felt that, as children, they had 'enough' rather than 'few' or 'lots' of toys (Papatheodorou 2010: 16). Qualitative evidence suggested that they had far fewer toys than children now and that many of these were handmade. Their choice of words is interesting as, according to Geraghty, offering 'too many [play] materials can be confusing and disconcerting to children' (1990: 193).

Practitioners have reported how some children in free flow settings just flit from one thing to another, not sure of what to focus on with so much available; this is exacerbated when inevitable time limitations apply. Anecdotally, on a trip to a museum children were free to explore at their own speed but they simply ran from one exhibit to another until they had seen everything. It was only then that they returned to those exhibits which held most appeal and spent the remainder of their visit examining these. At first sight the children's behaviour appeared disappointing, but with the benefit of hindsight it revealed a sophisticated strategy for ensuring that they got the most out of the time available and didn't miss anything amazing!

Space and scale

While much sensory-rich play involves exploration with the hands, meaningful interactions are also needed on a larger scale to provide full-bodied play and learning. The offer of sand, water and natural resources in small trays indoors is a valuable part of provision, but no substitute for children experiencing it in context and on a larger scale, in an ever-changing environment outdoors. Like the muddy puddle that magically appears after a downpour, or the dry patch of earth beneath the tree in an otherwise sodden garden, these natural scenarios are ripe for exploration and invite meaningful and holistic play. As practitioners in Norway discovered, the reverse is also the case, with small- and large-scale provision offering different qualities and appeal (Broadhead 2004). To maximize relevance and interest, plan any indoor and outdoor spaces with this in mind.

When I think about providing adequate space for children's play an image of a girl building a wooden block construction comes to mind (Community Playthings 2008). So large and sophisticated is her creation that the classroom has literally been subsumed by the structure! Although unrealistic in all but a few settings this reminds us of children's ability to think big and the importance of not imposing a glass ceiling by limiting time, space or the number of blocks available. It is easy to see how children typically offered small pieces of paper or small spaces for construction will limit their play to this scale. Returning to the concept of functional fixedness introduced in Chapter 3, this has important implications for the role and pedagogy of adults generally. If simply offering children open-ended play opportunities affects their ability to think creatively, then offering the reverse in the form of templates, jigsaw puzzles and didactic teaching will encourage convergent thinking (where there is only one answer). Although a useful and necessary part of everyday life, this needs to be balanced with divergent thinking opportunities if we are to foster creativity and problem-solving abilities. It is with this in mind that Stages 2 and 3 of the Continuum enable opportunities to offer the resources in a multitude of ways.

A supportive adult

Questions to consider

- Do you have any particular sensory preferences?
- Does the existing provision favour your own sensory preferences?
- Does your own attitude, experience, or 'phobias' currently limit sensory-rich play?

The emotional environment

Although the physical environment naturally springs to mind, its emotional counterpart is equally important. Geraghty describes the adult's role in creative play as involving 'an attitude which encourages curiosity, exploration, initiative, improvisation and provision of materials suited to the ages, stages, interests and needs of the children involved' (1990: 210). McInnes *et al.* suggest that in the same way that an enabling physical environment affords numerous play opportunities, 'social and emotional affordances' (2011: 123) are determined by the social interactions and emotional environment. A large tree in an outdoor area offers shelter, opportunities for climbing, foraging and hiding; a smooth surface affords play with tricycles and wheeled toys; and a patch of soil scope for making mud pies, exploring muddy puddles, looking at reflections and so much more. Similarly, several aspects of an adult's behaviour determine the culture or emotional environment and these are key to children's enjoyment of the physical environment.

Assumptions and expectations

If you have a particular interest, be it football, horses or *Eastenders*, you'll know that it is much easier sharing this interest with others who have the same passion. You don't need to explain the basics as they understand these and the appeal. The same can be said of sensory play. We will be much more willing to see the sensory potential of simple things; create time and opportunities for sensory play; encourage others to try it; understand its benefits and what it could do for them, if we actually experience and enjoy sensory play ourselves. We discovered in Chapters 4, 5 and 6 that children rarely need any explanation of how to play with open-ended resources like those found in a Treasure Basket, yet adults frequently dismiss deceptively 'simple' resources like these, oblivious to their widespread appeal and play potential. One such response was seen in an Activity Centre session:

> A 3-year-old boy appears at the door looking at the Treasure Baskets and sand arranged in the room. His mother peers in the room and quickly says, 'You're too old for it' as she moves away. The boy stays lingering at the door so I invite him to play. His mother agrees, reiterating that he's probably too old, and leaves him in the room to play.
>
> For the next hour he plays intently with the two Treasure Baskets, exploring the objects, finding matching objects, using them for a range of pretend play scenarios and problem solving. In the absence of his mother he sits for the majority of the time next to another adult, and throughout his play he initiates numerous interactions as he commentates on his play; asks for her help; exclaims loudly 'Look, two the same!' as he discovers two tea balls; and asks questions: 'Can you hear the noise?'

This observation is interesting on several levels.

- It reveals the flexibility and appeal of this resource for older children, showing that it does have something positive to offer in terms of age-appropriate play.
- It suggests that if a child is comfortable with adult presence, or, in this boy's case, actively seeks it, then perhaps they are better able to tolerate ill-timed or inappropriate interventions without disturbing the flow of play.
- It reveals children's innate drive to pursue learning tools, such as matching and pairing.
- It highlights the central role of the adult in this child's play. This takes me back to the pearls of wisdom of my own health visitor, 'You are your child's most important plaything' – a view certainly true of interactions with babies, but which permeates through 'good parenting' and is perhaps symptomatic of older children's need for adult engagement in play. We saw in Chapter 8 the importance of adults not imposing glass ceilings on children's learning and capabilities, particularly children with SEN. It is only natural to draw upon our own experiences and beliefs, but care needs to be taken to avoid unintentionally restricting learning opportunities, for example by limiting the time available for play.

Time

When reflecting upon the importance of time, Chilvers introduces the idea of children needing to 'wallow' – a wonderful word which truly conveys the dreamy essence of being a child (Chilvers, cited in White 2011). With increasingly mapped-out lives, after-school clubs and organized activities, even children can face the pressure of limited time (Play England 2011: 19). For some, sensory-rich play is about losing yourself in the moment, which can be at odds with the timetabling of the day. The importance of time is aptly demonstrated by the three 4-year-old children playing with sand in Chapter 7. Had the practitioner hurried their thinking, just how different might the outcomes have been? The children would have been deprived of this opportunity for sustained shared thinking; the learning less concrete without hands-on experimentation and peer mentoring; and the practitioner unaware of the depth of their understanding.

Forbes recognized the importance of giving babies adequate time with a Treasure Basket, not just because she observed them playing for up to an hour or more but because they needed time to acquaint themselves fully with the resource before engaging in meaningful play. Over four weekly sessions the nature of their play changed and levels of engagement significantly increased. While early sessions were typically rated by Forbes as 'low to moderate involvement' (Laevers *et al.* 1997), by the fourth week this had risen to 'high to extremely high' (2004: 91). In observations of children's play I have seen a similar 'warming-up stage' in action as children, particularly those older than 12 months, appear to get to grips with this strange yet captivating resource. Although in my experience this process typically takes minutes or hours rather than weeks, over a period of time a child's play will develop and change. This has important planning implications for practitioners if we are to avoid destroying one of the key attributes of this type of play, that of prolonged focus and concentration. We know that children, from across all ages, typically play with a Treasure Basket for an hour or more, yet often practitioners have admitted that they offer a Treasure Basket for only 20-minute sessions. As a consequence they may never have witnessed deeply engaged play and are less likely to be persuaded of its value.

The presence of adults

A key dimension of creating a positive emotional environment is how children perceive adults. You may have noticed how, in the presence of an adult, children's play can be very different. Alert to adult cues and any mismatch between their spoken word and body language, this can fundamentally alter the focus of children's play. McInnes *et al.* (2011) identified how children are well versed in sensing not only what they can and can't do but also what actions will please adults. Armitage (2004) discovered that 'children value the time spent away from adults and actively seek public areas that can offer this' (cited by Play England 2011: 19). Adults' vivid childhood play memories provide a cautionary reminder of what children enjoy and ultimately remember, and the presence of adults rarely features in accounts of den making, playing in the woods, or climbing trees (Papatheodorou 2010)!

Activity 25

Think about a vivid play memory from your childhood. Were any adults present and if so what role did they play in shaping or supporting play? Were they just on the periphery or did they actively become engaged in play? Did they successfully join in or did it feel as though they were trying to take over play? Does this offer any insight into your role in children's play?

For Elinor Goldschmied the presence of an adult was a key requirement during Treasure Basket play, therefore children's perception of the presence of an adult is of particular relevance to our focus. According to McInnes *et al.* (in relation to 'normal' play), children in several settings showed 'enhanced performance and behaviour' when an adult was nearby, rather than present during an activity. The results of a small-scale exploratory study compared adult role and behaviour in two foundation stage classrooms (Settings A and B), revealing marked differences in adult pedagogy and children's perception of play. In both settings the adults perceived their role to be one of observing play to understand play themes and purpose better. However, in Setting A practitioners saw themselves as 'play partners', recognizing that they don't always get it right: 'Sometimes I play alongside them, sometimes they don't want me beside them and they move away, that's okay' (McInnes *et al.* 2011: 127).

In Setting B, adults felt that the focus should be on learning rather than play; that they should only intervene in play if invited (which seldom happened); and that the pressures of time also limited their ability to get involved in play. The result was that children in Setting A were afforded more 'choice and control' (McInnes *et al.* 2011: 131) and did not associate the presence of an adult with 'work'. In Setting B, the presence of an adult, emphasis upon adult-led activities and minimal choice and control, signalled work rather than play to these children. Ironically this distinction between play and non-play was further compounded by adults not becoming involved in play, whereas in Setting A, their efforts to play alongside helped blur this distinction. Wood offers another dimension to this, suggesting the idea of a work–play continuum, with practitioners injecting playfulness into non-play activities (cited in Broadhead 2010: 21). Similarly Murray found a relationship between the frequency of children's explorations, the quality of these and the degree of adult structure in settings (2011: 13). As we have seen, the Sensory Play Continuum provides opportunities for introducing playfulness, choice and agency into this play–work conundrum.

Emotional cues

Research suggests that children are able to distinguish between play and non-play activities simply by an adult's approach and attitude. According to McInnes *et al.* children use a combination of environmental cues, such as location of an activity and adult involvement, and emotional cues, such as choice and the voluntary nature of the activity. Collectively this 'enables children to map activities on a play–work continuum' (2011: 123) and shapes their perception of 'social and emotional' affordances based on what is happening, who is participating and previous experiences of similar situations. So an activity on the floor (as opposed to at a table), with an adult nearby (instead of present), and choice available was characterized by better performance and learning conducive behaviours as well as being more likely to be described by children as play (McInnes *et al.* 2011: 124). This has important implications for Treasure Basket play and links closely to the adult's role in providing reassurance.

Providing reassurance

Forbes explored the role of both the adult and environment in supporting babies' interactions with a Treasure Basket. A baby girl was observed over a period of four weeks, with two other babies and her key person present. On several occasions the girl appeared anxious and needed adult reassurance (she was new to the setting). Initially this took the form of her key person picking her up and physically removing her from the area. Each time she returned to play with the basket, her key person sitting nearby. After reflection upon the nature of adult support provided, and the fact that practitioners were quick to pick her up and cuddle her for reassurance, it was agreed to see whether she could remain in situ with the basket, with her key person providing reassurance simply by stroking her back (Forbes 2004). Similarly, we saw in Chapter 7 how, when combined with appropriate adult support, a Treasure Basket became an invaluable tool for a child experiencing separation anxiety. The practitioner's body language conveyed warmth and interest without restricting the child's actions and this, together with the agenda-less resources, provided an anchor for her explorations. In other words, the Treasure Basket and practitioner functioning effectively together created an enabling environment.

Support

This brings us to the final role of the adult – that of supporting children's play and thinking through sensitive facilitation. Knowing when and when not to intervene in children's play is a difficult decision that even the most experienced practitioners don't always get right. In a Forest School session in the UK, two 4- to 5-year-old girls spent time collecting short, sawn-off branches from the forest floor, each approximately 30 cm long. They found two tree stumps to sit on and laid the lengths of wood on an upturned tree stump between the two of them. With focus and energy they vigorously rolled the branches backwards and forwards, with their palms flat and fingers outstretched, using a similar action to rolling pastry. I watched them deeply focused on the task in hand, waiting for a clearer insight into what they were doing. Their concentration was interrupted by a well-meaning practitioner asking, 'What are you doing girls?' They instantly stopped what they were doing and moved away from the logs, their play punctuated by the well-intended question. Having observed the play unfold I felt robbed, not knowing whether the children had been rolling pastry or something far removed. As for the children, one can only wonder what they felt and what might have been explored further.

The EPPE report (Sylva *et al.* 2004: 37) highlighted the importance of providing a balance between adult-led and child-led play, as well as group work and individual activities. Although based on play generally, this is equally relevant to sensory play. Best practice was found to embody ample opportunities for sustained interactions, the provision of challenge, and progression in children's thinking skills. Given appropriate spaces to foster such interactions, the time to fully explore new ideas, a supportive environment and sensitive adult involvement, children's thinking was found to blossom and grow. The EPPE report identified several factors for encouraging deeply satisfying, memory-making play:

- enabling differentiation and challenge;
- scaffolding learning to 'build bridges' between a child's knowledge and what they are 'capable of knowing' (Siraj-Blatchford and Sylva 2004: 9);
- the use of open-ended questions to stimulate and support rather than probe and test;

- encouragement of new experiences;
- adults watching and listening before making their own mark.

Sensory-rich play has much to offer by way of learning support, including its open-ended qualities that naturally differentiate and provide challenge; its ability to scaffold learning and provoke questions; the fact that there are no right or wrong ways to play; and the limitless opportunities for new experiences. In the hands of a skilled practitioner the potential is limitless, especially when attuned to the needs of the children and their own sensory perspective.

Exploring our own behaviour

Most of us experience some form of sensory intolerance or preference such as an aversion to the feel of gloop or sand, sopping wet clothes, or spinning on a roundabout, which we will respond to in our own unique ways. As a parent or practitioner we need to be careful not to convey this to the children within our care by subconsciously limiting sensory provision.

A word about safety and risk

Play in recent years has become characterized by an increasingly risk-averse culture. Adults can provide the safest possible play environment and if it is bland and unchallenging with limited play appeal children will naturally look for ways of altering it to make it more exciting. If you've ever seen children quickly tire of sliding down a slide in favour of walking up it or even attaching a rope to the top to climb up (as was repeatedly observed in a reception class playground); or insisting on walking, running and jumping from a roadside wall, you will have seen this for yourself. For adults too this rings true, with many childhood memories relaying exciting play experiences filled with challenge and risk, like wading in deep mud, climbing trees or building fires. Safety is of course essential, as is appropriate clothing and footwear, but a balance between protection and restriction is needed to avoid stifling some of the most enriching forms of play.

Many safety measures are common sense. When selecting objects for a Treasure Basket, first check the items for sharp edges and loose parts, which could cause a potential choking hazard. Regularly check the condition of play materials, replacing any that have become damaged. Frequently wash or clean objects with soapy water, avoiding harsh chemicals that could in themselves present a health hazard to children. Use common sense when children have streaming colds, by either avoiding use or limiting the objects to washable ones. Consider how best to equip children with the necessary knowledge and skills to take responsibility themselves, like knowing that a key part of Treasure Basket play is tidying away at the end; clearing up spillages that may cause a slipping hazard; and knowing where to access child-sized brushes and brooms for clearing up. Talk about what might happen if they take particular actions and how they can achieve the same thrill or effect in a safer way. Many children may do this subconsciously already, appraising play opportunities much like carrying out a risk assessment (Palmer 2010). In our risk-averse culture it is important to try to get the balance right, rather than unwittingly removing all the fun, excitement and challenge in the name of safety.

Activity 26

- Put your hand in a bag of typical Treasure Basket objects and feel them with your eyes closed. Write down any describing words that come to mind, like smooth, cold, hard, and so on. Your list will probably include words like 'bristly', 'pointy', 'sharp' or even 'scary', not words generally associated with children's toys. It may also include words like 'exciting', 'wow' or, as one practitioner in a training session described, a 'what can it be? object'. Repeat with a bag containing 'normal' toys. This time your list might include words like 'dull', 'safe' and 'boring', just some of the words identified by practitioners on training courses. It seems that the extra 'risk' of the unusual objects is rewarded by added excitement and surprise.
- Try to think of instances where children appear to have carried out their own 'assessment of risk' and changed action as a result? Next time you are faced with such a situation (if safe to do so), take a moment to try to understand what the child is thinking before rushing in to take action.

Supporting children's needs

Questions to consider

- Do individual children prefer or avoid particular sensory experiences?
- How can you best support all children's sensory needs?

We referred in Chapter 3 to children's interests and schemas generally and the importance of understanding these when planning provision. When it comes to children with sensory processing difficulties it is essential to be attuned to their particular sensory responses as well as being aware of our own preferences and dislikes in case these inadvertently limit sensory provision. Key to this will be analysing children's behaviour with a view to diagnosing problems, respecting sensory coping mechanisms and exploring your own actions.

Diagnosing problems

Analysing children's actions to understand sensory triggers and determine what can be easily changed or improved within the environment is a key aspect of the adult's role. Biel and Peske (2009) poignantly describe this from years of personal experience, but given that we are all likely to experience some form of sensory difficulty, albeit not to an extent that detracts from daily life, the following advice should help support any child within your care.

> When you stop to analyse a situation or task that your child has trouble with, there's almost always something you can alter. Think about the noise, the sounds, the smells, the tastes, the sights, the movements your child must make. Is there anything you can modify in the environment to improve things? What can be done in a different way?
>
> (2009: 136)

Respecting children's capabilities and needs

Children's responses to sensory stimulation impact upon their ability to participate in play, learning and life. With this in mind a number of positive actions were suggested in Chapter 8 for improving the benefits of Treasure Baskets and resources generally. To plan effectively for children's needs, we need to understand and respect these and be aware of our expectations of what children can achieve within an enabling environment. Staff at a Children's Centre experienced a learning journey, gaining a better understanding of children's capabilities and pushing the boundaries of what they felt acceptable in terms of risk and challenge. In doing so they re-evaluated their expectations of children with SEN. An observation of teenagers playing with a Treasure Basket in a special school revealed similar results. They freely engaged with the objects and, to the surprise of practitioners, examples of sensory regulation (using objects to achieve a 'just right' state) and imaginative play emerged. Throughout the book we have witnessed something of children's brilliance. We have also seen how our pedagogical approach can inadvertently limit their capabilities by constraining scale, creativity, space, time and risk. We will now consider the thorny issue of adult involvement in play.

Adult behaviour

A key challenge for adults observing children's play is deciding if, when and how to intervene. Any decision on this should be shaped by practitioners' knowledge of the environment, children's needs and the nature of the relationship. For many parents, active involvement in a child's play is synonymous with the support and encouragement that they provide as part of 'good parenting'. Observing 20 Treasure Basket sessions at an Activity Centre, it has become clear to me that the parents or carers who accompany their child in a session typically take an active interest by commentating on their play ('you've picked up . . .' or 'you made a loud bang'); asking a question, generally closed (e.g. 'what is it?'); or suggesting a particular course of action (e.g. 'try banging . . .'). Some parents model certain behaviours and activities instead of verbalizing them, such as upturning pots and banging them with a utensil or making a mixing motion to inspire domestic role-play, but most interventions are verbalized. A small minority simply watched play, while a larger number talked with other adults, only getting involved in the event of disruptive play.

Generally speaking, adult behaviour could be divided into those actions or behaviours that support play and those that do not. Responding positively to the resource, watching in silence, sitting nearby, smiling and giving reassurance or praise if needed, asking open-ended questions and subtle actions were found to be most effective in supporting play. An example of one such subtle action was provided by a grandfather who sat near a Treasure Basket to watch his grandson play. When the 3-year-old quickly got up to move away, rather than immediately following, he picked up a spoon and gently tapped it on the edge of the metal bucket to attract the child's attention. This action alone, without any words, was enough for the boy to come back and sit down to play with the objects. Later, when the boy had moved to the container of sand and his attention waned, the grandfather gently swirled a metal pot containing dry sand, couscous and rice. The larger grains rose to the top and made a gentle noise. The boy looked at the pot saying 'noise', then resumed play. Still later the grandfather provided encouragement as his grandson used a spoon to fill a tin with dried couscous, sand, rice, glitter and alphabet pasta. He said in a singsong voice, 'It's getting fuller and fuller and fuller' in time with the boy's careful actions.

Agency and control

Geraghty suggests that

> As children touch, smell and look, the adult helps them to verbalize the experience and thus gain more understanding of what they have

done . . . Intervention as to content or techniques can stunt and stultify the exploration essential to satisfaction with the medium.
(Geraghty 1990: 210)

In Chapter 7 we glimpsed the absorbing play of three 4-year-olds when deeply engaged in play with objects and sand. Some may argue that failure to get involved in this session missed a valuable opportunity to extend play and learning further. To my mind the practitioner got it right, leaving it to the three peers to reach the zone of proximal development, supported by each other and the resources. The deep level of involvement, I would suggest 'extremely high' (Laevers *et al.* 1997), would potentially have been punctuated by adult intervention. This could so easily have shattered the fragile balance of control of these 4-year-olds, robbing them either of their hands-on discoveries or their sense of being able to solve problems on their own. The practitioner in this instance chose to watch and learn; better informed of the children's grasp of the world, she then built on the learning observed by incorporating more opportunities to explore different properties in subsequent sessions.

When adults do get involved, the relationship between adult and child, emotional environment, cues and pedagogy appears to come to the fore in limiting any potential disturbance to play. This reveals the delicate balancing act involved in every intervention. Take this example of children's play with the Treasure Basket objects and some sand in a Children's Centre:

> Two boys take the chain from the basket and put it in the sand. Together they push and pull the chain in the sand. Other children come over to watch. 'WOW' exclaims one little boy, 'it's a snake, it's a snake, it's a snake in the desert!' Another boy says, 'Yeah yeah and he's looking for food.' They move it along the sand and the practitioner says, 'What do snakes do?' and the group of children gathered start hissing as the chain is pushed into the sand.

The adult's intervention in the form of a question may easily have backfired, interrupting play, but instead, perhaps because she was in tune with the play and so the question was relevant or because the chosen question was open rather than closed, the adult's intervention seems to add an extra dimension to the play instead. Intervention is not always the best course of action, as we can see with the benefit of hindsight in the following nursery observation:

> J (aged 2 years and 10 months) holds a metal bowl and puts a small marble elephant figure into the bowl. He shakes the bowl so that it makes a noise. An adult asks, 'What are you doing there J?' He replies, 'Jumping.' J is asked to take a photo of his 'toy'. The adult

shows J how to use the camera and the adult asks, 'Who do you want to show your photo to?' He replies with a practitioner's name.

Rather than practitioners just observing play, the setting wanted to give children a more meaningful role as researchers, recording their views through photography. Unfortunately this backfires as the technology gets in the way and this, together with the practitioner's question, interrupts the observation. Ironically in a test run with pretend cameras the children started photographing objects without any prompting!

Adult involvement in play

With a few exceptions, ironically those children who were left to attend Treasure Basket sessions without their carer were able to play more freely with the resources without interruption or guidance. So herein lies the rub: a fundamental rift between what is perceived as good parenting (staying with the child and being actively involved) and quality play. Well-meaning interruptions can actually stifle children's play by encouraging a particular kind of play; giving the message that the adult's ideas are better than the child's; or suppressing children's creativity and imagination. Hughes suggests that the last quarter of the twentieth century has

> seen the appearance of a variety of new forms of play materials that are highly structured, highly complicated and technology-advanced. Such toys appear to encourage activity that might be more accurately referred to as 'entertainment' than as spontaneous play, and they often substitute the imagination of their creators for those of the children who interact with them

> (2003: 8)

He blames interactive toys for changing the focus of children's play. Instead of children asking, 'What can I do with this?' as described in Chapter 4, they typically ask instead, 'What does this toy do?' In a culture where toys do things rather than being the product of a child's hands or imagination it is unsurprising perhaps that 'good parenting' is seen as providing the interaction and support needed.

In one Treasure Basket session described by a practitioner, several children from babies to 4-year-olds were sitting around a Treasure Basket. The babies instantly reached into the basket and began exploring, not needing any explanation of how to play. However, the older children turned to their carers who were behind them, looking bemused by the basket of objects. No clearer of what the resource was or how to play with it they simply shrugged their shoulders. The children turned back to the Treasure Basket and watched the babies playing, before following their lead and picking up objects to explore. As one would expect of older children encountering this type of resource for the first time, their play evolved, moving through the different stages of play with a Treasure Basket, but at an accelerated pace.

Getting the balance right

The EPPE research revealed the importance of providing a balance between adult-led and child-led activities in the early years (Sylva *et al.* 2004: 37). Research has revealed that many practitioners are acutely aware of the value of play generally, and of providing plenty of opportunities for child-led play; however, as Moyles and Worthington (2011) discovered, this is not always reflected in practice. Bernstein provides a useful framework for understanding pedagogy, suggesting that **classification** denotes how clearly defined or merged different subjects are and **framing** 'the relationship between teacher and pupil and the degree of control between them' (1996 in McInnes *et al.* 2011: 122). Strong framing, whereby control rests with the teacher, and clear classification where the boundaries between different subjects are clear, are characteristic of traditional didactic teaching. In contrast, weak framing and weak boundaries are more typical of early years settings. There are key links between parents' typical behaviours during play and classification and framing. In the quest for a balance between adult-led and child-led play, practitioners need to plot a course between these two extremes, and may find the Sensory Play Continuum helpful in doing so.

Adults' role in the Sensory Play Continuum

For practitioners unsure of whether and when to intervene, the Sensory Play Continuum provides a useful framework for exploring adults' role in children's play. As Figure 9.2 shows, this can be seen in terms of adults' direct and indirect involvement. As children move through the Continuum, the balance between adult and child is not rigid and stilted but fluid with almost dance-like qualities. Much like a conversation between equals, the delicate balance between adult and child initiation, and consequent enrichment of play, are apparent.

Flexibility and the continuum

A key aspect of practitioners' skill set is about understanding children's needs. This led to the decision by one reception class teacher to change the order in

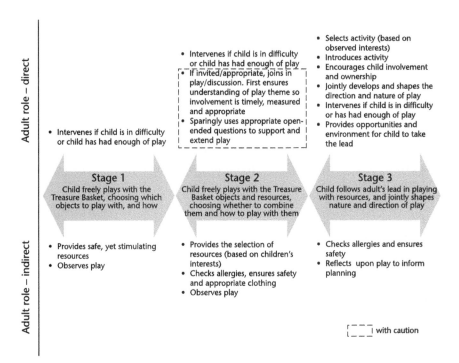

Figure 9.2 Adults' role in the Sensory Play Continuum

which she introduced the three stages of the Sensory Play Continuum. Sensing that the children were not ready for unstructured play, because they were still learning to treat resources with respect generally, she decided to introduce the Treasure Basket via Stage 3, a structured activity. She selected an activity which involved sorting the objects according to criteria and the children, aged 4–5 years, sat in a circle on the floor as the basket was passed around the group.

> The children talked about the Treasure Basket objects and used a range of senses to describe them, such as the smell of dried orange, feel of the cloth. The children then sorted the objects using their own criteria. Some chose colour or size. As a teacher-led group the qualities of hard/soft and rough/smooth were chosen and there was lots of good discussion and reasoning and thoughtful suggestions on how best to classify the items on a large Venn diagram on the floor.

Although this session might seem somewhat didactic and staged relative to free exploration, within the context of formal school-based approaches to learning it was practical, hands-on and fun. Unfortunately, due to the brevity of observation records (Papatheodorou 2010), it is not possible to determine the level of children's engagement (in terms of numbers of children and depth of involvement); the degree to which they were contributing; and whether the children's choices were the views of the majority or the few, but the activity was popular with children asking to play with the Treasure Basket again.

Another essential requirement in executing Stage 3 is responding flexibly to children's cues. When Child R and his peers were not engaged in building the three pigs' houses the practitioner followed their lead by responding flexibly. Ironically, by freeing them up to pursue their own discoveries, the practitioner enabled Child R to return to the story, using the objects to re-enact it in an episode of quality compositional play.

Activity 27

Follow the different stages of the Continuum (set out in Chapter 3), noticing how your role changes at each stage, and which elements remain constant. Think about other types of play that you observe, support or actively participate in, and for each of these reflect upon your evolving role.

Observations and planning

Key in the role of the adult is appreciating Treasure Basket play for what it is rather than judging and assigning value to every aspect of play. That said, observational records are essential for analysing existing provision, reflecting upon the needs of the individual child and assessing levels of engagement. When writing observations we need to be careful not to impose our own interpretations of play. Where we do feel it is appropriate to add extra comments, perhaps to flag up areas to consider, these should be distinguished (as I have) by using square brackets. Clearly, meaningful judgements can only be made if observational records are sufficiently detailed to enable proper reflection. Furthermore, we have seen how children's play develops, and interests and schemas may underlie these changes – it is only by reflecting upon a sequence of observations that these patterns of play become apparent and truly enabling environments can be planned. The sensory environment is not static but ever changing, therefore it is important to continuously review provision and needs rather than viewing a sensory appraisal as a one-off process. This also provides an opportunity to assess the impact of any actions taken. As we saw in Chapter 7, play with a Treasure Basket at any of the Continuum stages can yield positive curriculum outcomes. For children, as agents of their own play, it is essential that learning is relevant, real and fun. With careful observation-led planning, collections of simple objects and environments can deliver curriculum outputs without the need for silo-based learning.

Putting it all together

In Chapter 1 and throughout the book we have alluded to the vital but changing role of the adult in supporting and extending children's play. This chapter has crystallized what this might look like in practice, focusing on the three ingredients of providing an enabling environment (physically and emotionally), identifying children's specific needs and recognizing adults' direct and indirect input. Although useful for focusing attention, in reality a balance needs to be achieved between each of these, as an enabling environment can only be created with the right resources, space, time, culture and support. Research has explored the relationship between a print-rich environment and children's reading ability, suggesting that when allied with a supportive adult using rich and appropriate language a print-rich environment contributes towards improved reading. Could it similarly be hypothesized that a sensory-rich environment coupled with a supportive, enthusiastic adult could offer similar sensory gains? In the final chapter readers will be invited to draw their own conclusion on the value of sensory-rich play.

10 Conclusion: Treasure Baskets – a twenty-first century resource?

Despite their parents' best efforts at stopping them, children commonly jump into mud puddles, play with their food, climb on the furniture, and jump on the beds. The multisensory nature of their play provides the ingredients necessary for the alchemy that promotes development.

(Smith Roley *et al.*, *Understanding the Nature of Sensory Integration with Diverse Populations*)

Overview

In this final chapter we pull together the key threads of the book and the insight this has provided into children as agents of their play. Given the opportunity, children will discover wonder, excitement and enrichment everywhere, from a muddy puddle to a cool shady spot beneath a tree, or in the cosy indoors. This book gives a mere taster of the importance of our senses as a gateway to all learning and how objects, such as those found in a Treasure Basket, provide the key for literally making sense of the world.

Children are intuitively driven to follow their bodies' natural urges to explore different schema, look for novelty and satisfy their thirst for sensory-rich experiences or, conversely, to avoid unwelcome stimuli. Not only are the senses vital for learning, but they shape our very essence as sensory beings, impacting upon our ability to function effectively in everyday life. Returning to the six 'dimensions of beyond' underpinning this book, we will now consider these in turn.

The importance of sensory play

From the feast of sensory-rich play on offer, I have provided a snapshot of the resources and environments available to a playful individual. More importantly, this book offers a fresh perspective on the importance of play with objects, something often overlooked, as this unlocks the key to play with just about anything! The delicate interplay between adult, child and environment has been explored and we have seen how, depending upon the physical and emotional environment and needs of the individual child, sensory play can provide a highly motivating, exciting and uplifting stimulus or a deeply calming experience. The ever-changing qualities of play, its open-ended potential and ability to inspire awe, help explain something of the appeal of sensory play. The Sensory Play Continuum offers a framework for realizing the full potential of sensory-rich play.

Understanding babies' brains

I began this book in the knowledge that play is changing (Papatheodorou 2010: 26), with fewer opportunities for children to play freely outside, more competing interests on their ever-decreasing time, the appeal of screen-based alternatives and a heightened awareness of stranger danger. Given children's greater detachment from the environment, sensory-rich play instinctively makes sense, but it is only by focusing on the complex interplay between the senses that we can truly appreciate the wonder of babies' brains. 'Everything we know about the world and ourselves has come through our senses' (Bogdashina 2003: 37). A baby's body and brain are hard-wired to search out novelty and pattern, interact with the environment, and like scientists, fine-tune their understanding of the world. Having undertaken countless Treasure Basket observations I intuitively felt play with objects to be beneficial to development. We have not only discovered that traditional views of babies are misguided, but also learnt about the fundamental role played by objects in decoding the world and providing the foundations for lifelong learning.

The benefits and appeal of objects

In researching this book I have furthered my quest for the underlying appeal of the Treasure Basket. Simple objects offer infinite opportunities for refining infants' thinking and developing imagination. When offered in conjunction with the Sensory Play Continuum, these possibilities increase exponentially, providing fertile ground for developing complex neural connections. To date links between neuroscience and education have been scarce. If we are to provide firm foundations for future pedagogy and practice, knowledge between these two fields must flow. Closely related to this is the importance of credible research to test and substantiate thinking. Many points have been raised afresh in this book and practitioners are invited to get involved in research to expand our knowledge further.

Benefits of Treasure Basket play to older children

As the emphasis upon play looks set to be subsumed within a push for 'school readiness' in the UK, bringing the curriculum to life with hands-on sensory-rich play and learning will become increasingly important. I suggested in Chapter 4 that Treasure Baskets may have wrongly become synonymous with heuristic play, a confusion stemming from the fact that the latter is both a way of playing and a type of resource. Clearly they both share a focus on play with objects (as does loose parts play), but a Treasure Basket is a sensory-rich collection of eclectic objects and heuristic play an eclectic collection of similar objects. They differ not just in sensory appeal but also in scale. Although intended for different aged children, the distinction in type of play has somewhat blurred, with older children now accessing Treasure Baskets for heuristic and pretend play. Offering a Treasure Basket to older children is a clear departure from Goldschmied's thinking, as is the Sensory Play Continuum. My belief is that to restrict or prescribe would be at odds not just with the essence of sensory play, but with the underlying message written in children's absorption.

With a potential narrowing of the curriculum practitioners will need to tap into their creativity to introduce opportunities for enriching learning. We have seen the ability of Treasure Basket objects to captivate and transfix children and these same principles can be applied to the world of books. By gathering a sensory-rich collection of objects this can help bring stories to life. In Chapter 4 we discovered a key potential benefit of Treasure Basket play, that of mixed ages engaging with the same resource in their own age-appropriate way. The same can be said of sensory-rich artefacts used to enhance a story. Like the objects in a Treasure Basket selected for their special sensorial qualities and wow factor, the key thing is to pick the right story with the potential to engage children across the ages, and unusual objects that fit with the ethos of the Treasure Basket rather than obsessing about replicas of story characters. Like Child R (Chapter 6) who re-enacted the story using a knitted teddy rather than the wolf character that had been provided, artefacts like these have greater play potential, leaving more scope for a child's verdant imagination.

Child-led and/versus adult-led play

As parents we tend to marvel at the major milestones of sitting, walking and talking and often take for granted the enormity of children's everyday actions and learning. As we have discovered, behind these apparently simple actions lies a multitude of smaller milestones, each one essential for proceeding to the next. An understanding of the value of play with objects is crucial to engendering respect for Treasure Baskets. We have seen how involvement in children's play is for some synonymous with good parenting, but in reality can detract from quality play. The Sensory Play Continuum, born out of observations of children's play, provides a tool for achieving an all-important balance between adult and child-led play – a dynamic with dance-like qualities.

Exploring our sensory preferences

This book unpicks the vital role of the adult in creating an enabling environment and invites reflection of our own attitudes and sensory preferences, a learning journey which I have enjoyed taking in rediscovering sensory-rich play myself. As the importance of providing play outdoors has gained popularity in the early years sector, children's access to play in natural areas with limited adult involvement has declined. This reduction in play in unstructured 'wild spaces' has important implications for early years settings in terms of what is offered, where and how. This is also relevant to practitioners themselves who may not have accessed these types of play opportunities or share vivid childhood memories of exploration, challenge and escapism. For those children of the technological age for whom a box of buttons or pots and pans and utensils have no currency, sensory-rich play is somewhat alien or marginalized as messy play for 'special' days. With these patterns of play becoming entrenched and generational changes occurring, it is wonderful that a resource as simple and cheaply available as a special collection of objects can help to redress the balance, providing children with much-needed sensory stimulation. Of course, essential to this is adults recognizing the value of this type of play, reconnecting with the awe and wonder of objects in the hands of a playful individual.

In this technologically abundant age, adults are urged to re-evaluate play opportunities; watch children's innately driven explorations; take the lead from their play; and reconnect with the richness and benefits of deeply satisfying sensory play themselves. Like play itself, the value of Treasure Baskets as a twenty-first-century play resource is plain to see.

Appendix 1
Treasure Basket observation template

Child's name:	Age:	Have played with a Treasure Basket before? YES/NO	Date:	Start time:	Finish time:

Action to object(s) — Description

Please tick a column <u>every time</u> you observe each behaviour

√ √ √ √ √ √ √ √ √ √ √

Movement-related behaviour/activity

Behaviour	Description
Placing	Moving an object from place to place
Piling	Placing one object on top of another
Sequencing	Doing/arranging things one after another
Picking up object	Reaching for/selecting objects
Dropping object	Accidentally or on purpose
Rolling	Rolling the object with hand
Throwing	Throwing the object
Holding object with both hands	Using both hands to hold the same object
Transferring object from hand to hand	Passing the object from one hand to the other
Shaking object	Shaking or waving the object
Transporting or carrying	With body or in another container

Explorative behaviour/activity

Behaviour	Description
Pairing and matching	Noticing two things are the same
Sorting	Grouping or arranging objects
Mouthing	Putting object to mouth
Using two objects together	Combining objects in different ways
Using their feet with object(s)	Using feet to hold/touch object
Exploring	Using eyes and/or fingers to explore
Observing objects roll or fall	Noticing and watching an object fall or roll
Smelling	Obviously smelling or noticing smell

Manipulation

Squeezing or rubbing — Squeezing or rubbing the object
Manipulating the object — Moving any moveable parts
Turning with hands — To see or mouth a different part

Sound-making activities

Banging — Banging an object against another
Making noise with objects — Exploring sound making with objects

Communication

Babbling/speaking about their actions — As if commentating on play
Looking to carer — To smile/show/for reassurance
Wiggling feet with excitement/delight — Revealing excitement or delight

Problem-solving activities

Putting an object inside another — Enclosing or enveloping objects
Other

Pretend play

Domestic role-play — Cooking, cleaning, etc.
Fantasy play — Superheroes, princesses or story-making

References

Anderson, M. *et al.* (1962) *Activity Methods for Children Under Eight.* London: Evans Brothers.

Antle, A.N. (2012) Exploring how children use their hands to think: an embodied interactional analysis. Available at http://www.antle.iat.sfu.ca/publications.php [accessed 3 January 2012].

Ayres, A.J. (1972) *Sensory Integration and Learning Disorders.* Los Angeles, CA: Western Psychological Services.

Ayres, A.J. (2005) *Sensory Integration and the Child: Understanding Hidden Sensory Challenges.* Los Angeles, CA: Western Psychological Services.

Baillargeon, R. (2002) The acquisition of physical knowledge in infancy: a summary in eight lessons, in U. Goswami (ed.) (2002) *Blackwell Handbook of Childhood Cognitive Development.* Oxford: Blackwell Publishing.

Barton, J. and Pretty, J. (2010) What is the best dose of nature and green exercise for improving mental health? A multi-study analysis, *Environmental Science & Technology,* 44(10): 3947–55.

Beaver, M., Brewster, J. and Keene, A. (1997) *Child Care and Education for CCE and NVQ2.* Cheltenham: Stanley Thornes.

Biel, M.A. and Peske, N. (2009) *Raising a Sensory Smart Child,* revised edn. New York: Penguin Books.

Bilton, H. (2010) *Outdoor Learning in the Early Years,* 3rd edn. Abingdon: Routledge.

Bishop, J. (2001). Creating places for living and learning, in L. Abbott and C. Nutbrown, *Experiencing Reggio Emilia: Implications for Pre-school Provision.* Buckingham: Open University Press.

Bogdashina, O. (2003) *Sensory Perceptual Issues in Autism and Asperger Syndrome.* London: Jessica Kingsley Publishers.

Bornstein, M.H. and Mash, C. (2010) Experience-based and on-line categorization of objects in early infancy, *Child Development,* May/June 2010, 81(2): 884–97.

Brace, N. and Pike, G. (2005) Recognition, in N. Braisby and A. Gellatly (eds) (2005) *Cognitive Psychology.* Oxford: Oxford University Press in association with the Open University.

Braisby, N. (2005) Concepts, in N. Braisby and A. Gellatly (eds) (2005) *Cognitive Psychology.* Oxford: Oxford University Press in association with the Open University.

Brett-Green, B.A., Miller, L.J., Schoen, S.A. and Nielsen, D.M. (2010) An exploratory event-related potential study of multisensory integration in sensory over-responsive children, *Brain Research*, 1321: 67–77.

Brierley, J. (1994) *Give Me a Child Until He is Seven*, 2nd edn. London: The Falmer Press.

Broadhead, P. (2004) *Early Years Play and Learning*. London: Routledge Falmer.

Broadhead, P. (2010) *Play and Learning in the Early Years*. London: Sage Publications.

Brown, F. (2009) Playwork, in A. Brock, S. Dodds, P. Jarvis and Y. Olusoga (2009) *Perspectives on Play*. Harlow: Pearson.

Bruner, J.S., Jolly, A. and Sylva, K. (eds) (1976) *Play: Its Role in Development and Evolution*. Harmondsworth: Penguin Books.

Bryant, P. and Nuñes, T. (2002) *Children's Understanding of Mathematics*, in U. Goswami (ed.) (2002) *Blackwell Handbook of Childhood Cognitive Development*. Oxford: Blackwell Publishing.

Bundy, A.C., Shia, S., Qi, L. and Miller, L.J. (2007) How does sensory processing dysfunction affect play? *The American Journal of Occupational Therapy*, March/April, 61(2): 201–8.

Butterworth, G. and Harris, M. (1994) *Principles of Developmental Psychology*. Hove: Psychology Press.

Carlson-Finnerty, L. and Wartik, N. (1993) *Memory and Learning*. New York: Chelsea House Publishers.

Carter, R. (1998) *Mapping the Mind*. London: Phoenix.

Chilvers, D. (2011) As long as they need: the vital role of time, in J. White (ed.) (2011) *Outdoor Provision in the Early Years*. London: Sage Publications.

Community Playthings (2008) *Simple Materials – Rich Experiences* [DVD]. Roberts bridge: Community Products (UK).

Crowe, B. (1983) *Play is a Feeling*. London: Unwin Paperbacks.

Danks, F. and Schofield, J. (2005) *Nature's Playground*. London: Frances Lincoln.

DFE (2011) *Reforming the Early Years Foundation Stage (EYFS): Government Response to Consultation*. London: DFE.

DFE (2012) *Statutory Framework for the Early Years Foundation Stage* (EYFS) London: DFE.

Emmons, P.G. and Anderson, L.M. (2005) *Understanding Sensory Dysfunction: Learning, Development and Sensory Dysfunction in Autism Spectrum Disorders, ADHD, Learning Disabilities and Bipolar Disorder*. London: Jessica Kingsley.

Evans, G.W. and Wells, N.M. (2003) *Nearby Nature: A Buffer of Life Stress among Rural Children*. Available at http://eab.sagepub.com/cgi/content/abstract/35/3/311 [accessed 5 April 2009].

Exploratory Play (2006) [DVD] Newcastle upon Tyne: Siren Films.

Featherstone, S. and Williams, L. (2009) *The Sensory World: Progression in Play for Babies and Children*. London: A&C Black.

Fein, G. (1975) A transformational analysis of pretending, *Developmental Psychology*, 11: 291–6.

Forbes, R. (2004) *Beginning to Play*. Maidenhead: Open University Press.

Fox, J.E. (2011) *Back-to-Basics: Play in Early Childhood*. Available at http://www.earlychildhoodnews.com/earlychildhood/article_view. aspx?ArticleID=240 [accessed 25 September 2011].

Garvey, C. (1986) *Play*, 5th impression. Glasgow: Fontana Press.

Gascoyne, S. (2009) *Introducing Treasure Baskets*. Training handout. Available at http://www.playtoz.co.uk [accessed 12 May 2012].

Gascoyne, S. (2010) Observation summaries and comments. Unpublished paper.

Gascoyne, S. (2011) *Play in the EYFS: Sensory Play*. London: Practical Pre-School Books.

Geraghty, P. (1990) *Caring for Children*. Revised 2nd edn. London: Baillière Tindall.

Gergely, G. (2002) The development of understanding self and agency, in U. Goswami (ed.) (2002) *Blackwell Handbook of Childhood Cognitive Development*. Oxford: Blackwell Publishing.

Gibson, J.J. (1979) *The Ecological Approach to Visual Perception*. Mahwah, NJ: Lawrence Erlbaum Associates.

Gill, T. (2011) *Free Range Kids: Why Children Need Simple Pleasures and Everyday Freedom, and What We Can Do About It*. Dairylea Campaign for Simple Fun. Available at www.dairyleasimplefunreport.co.uk/pdf [accessed 7 March 2012].

Goddard, S.A. (1996) *A Teacher's Window Into the Child's Mind*. Eugene, OR: Fern Ridge Press.

Goldschmied, E. (1987) *Infants at Work* [DVD]. London: National Children's Bureau.

Goldschmied, E. and Jackson, S. (1994) *People Under Three*. London: Routledge.

Goswami, U. (2002) Inductive and deductive reasoning, in U. Goswami (ed.) (2002) *Blackwell Handbook of Childhood Cognitive Development*. Oxford: Blackwell Publishing.

Grainger, T., Burnard, P. and Craft, A. (2007) Examining possibility thinking in action in early years settings. Paper presented at Imaginative Education Research Symposium, 12–15 July 2006, Vancouver.

Hamer, R. D. (1990) *What Can My Baby See?* Revised by Giuseppe Mirabella. Available at http://www.ski.org/Vision/babyvision.html [accessed 13 March 2012].

Hannaford, C. (1995) *Smart Moves: Why Learning is Not All In Your Head.* Marshall, NC: Great Ocean Publishers.

Hill, J. (2010) What influence can regular, unstructured, wild, outdoor experiences have on children with additional needs?, in *Proceedings of the 2010 EECERA Conference.* Birmingham: EECERA.

Howard-Jones, P. (2007) Neuroscience and Education: Issues and Opportunities. Available at http://www.tlrp.org/index.html [accessed 13 March 2012].

Hughes, A.M. (2006) *Developing Play for the Under 3s.* London: David Fulton Publishers.

Hughes, A.M. (2009) *Problem Solving, Reasoning and Numeracy in the Early Years Foundation Stage.* Abingdon: Routledge.

Hughes, A.M. (2010) *Developing Play for the Under 3s.* 2nd edn. Abingdon: Routledge.

Hughes, F.P. (2003) *Spontaneous Play in the 21st Century.* Greenwich, CT: Information Age Publishing.

Kalliala, M. (2006) *Play Culture in a Changing World.* Maidenhead: Open University Press.

Kelman, K., Lindon, J. and Sharp, A. (2001) *Play and Learning for the Under 3s.* London: TSL Education.

Khan, C. (2011) Excitement and engagement: exploration into EEG rhythms in preshool children at rest and at play. Unpublished research paper, University of Hertfordshire.

Klatzky, R. L. and Lederman, S. J. (2002) Touch, in A.F. Healy and R.W. Proctor (eds) *Experimental Psychology,* Volume 4 in I. B. Weiner (Editor-in-Chief) *Handbook of Psychology.* New York: Wiley.

Kuo, F.E. and Taylor, A.F. (2004) A potential natural treatment for attention-deficit/hyperactivity disorder: evidence from a national study, *American Journal of Public Health,* 94(9): 1580–6.

Kurtz, A. (2006) *Visual Perception Problems in Children with AD/HD, Autism, and Other Learning Disabilities.* London: Jessica Kingsley Publishers.

Laevers, F., Vandenbussche, E., Kog, M. and Depondt, L. (1997) *A Process-oriented Child Monitoring System for Young Children.* Experiential Education Series, No. 2. Leuven: Centre for Experiential Education.

Lederman, S.J. and Klatzky, R.L. (1987) Hand movements: a window into haptic object recognition, *Cognitive Psychology,* 19: 342–8.

Liben, L.S. (2002) Spatial development in childhood: where are we now?, in U. Goswami (ed.) (2002) *Blackwell Handbook of Childhood Cognitive Development.* Oxford: Blackwell Publishing.

Lillard, A. (2002) Pretend play and cognitive development, in U. Goswami (ed.) (2002) *Blackwell Handbook of Childhood Cognitive Development.* Oxford: Blackwell Publishing.

Lindon, J., Kelman, K. and Sharp, A. (2001) *Play and Learning for the Under 3s.* London: TSL Education.

Louv, R. (2005) *Last Child in the Woods: Saving Our Children from Nature-Deficit Disorder.* Chapel Hill, NC: Algonquin Books.

McInnes, K., Crowley, K., Howard, J. and Miles, G. (2011) Differences in practitioners' understanding of play and how this influences pedagogy and children's perceptions of play, *Early Years*, 31(2): 121–33.

Macintyre, C. (2005) *Identifying Additional Learning Needs.* Abingdon: Routledge.

Macintyre, C. (2010) *Play for Children with Special Needs.* Abingdon: David Fulton Publishers.

Matterson, E.M. (1975) *Play with a Purpose for Under-Sevens.* Harmondsworth: Penguin Books.

May-Benson, T.A., Koomar, J.A. and Teasdale, A. (2009) Incidence of pre-, peri-, and post-natal birth and developmental problems of children with sensory processing disorder and children with autism spectrum disorder, *Frontiers in Integrative Neuroscience*, November, 3(31).

Meade, A. and Cubey, P. (2008) *Thinking Children: Learning About Schemas.* Maidenhead: Open University Press.

Meltzoff, A.N. (2002) Imitation as a mechanism of social cognition: origins of empathy, theory of mind, and the representation of action, in U. Goswami (ed.) (2002) *Blackwell Handbook of Childhood Cognitive Development.* Oxford: Blackwell Publishing.

Menzel, E.W. Jr (1976) Responsiveness to objects in free-ranging Japanese monkeys, in J.S. Bruner, A. Jolly and K. Sylva (eds) (1976) *Play – Its Role in Development and Evolution.* Harmondsworth: Penguin Books.

Miller, L.J., Nielsen, D.M., Schoen, S.A. and Brett-Green, B.A. (2009) Perspectives on sensory processing disorder: a call for translational research, *Frontiers in Integrative Neuroscience*, 3(22).

Mooney, C.G. (2000) *Theories of Childhood.* St Paul, MN: Redleaf Press.

Moxon, D. (2000) *Memory.* Jordan Hill: Heinemann Educational.

Moyles, J. and Worthington, M. (2011) The Early Years Foundation Stage through the daily experiences of children, TACTYC Occasional Paper No. 1. np: TACTYC.

Moyles, J.R. (1989) *Just Playing?* Buckingham: Open University Press.

Murray, J. (2011) Young children's explorations: young children's research?, *Early Child Development and Care*, 1–17. London: Routledge. DOI: 10.1080/03004430.2011.604728.

Oates, J. (ed.) (1979) *Early Cognitive Development.* London: Open University Press/Croom Helm.

Palmer, S. (2010) *Out to Play* [internet blog]. Available at: http://www.suepalmer.co.uk/modern_childhood_info_out_to.php [accessed 1 May 2012].

Papatheodorou, T. (2010) Sensory play. Unpublished paper, Anglia Ruskin University.

Pepler, D.J. and Ross, H.S. (1981) The effects of play on convergent and divergent problem solving, *Child Development*, 52: 1202–10.

Pike, G. and Edgar, G. (2005) Perception, in N. Braisby and A. Gellatly (eds) (2005) *Cognitive Psychology*. Oxford: Oxford University Press in association with the Open University.

Play England (2011) *A World Without Play: A Literature Review*. London: Play England.

Pound, L. (2006) *How Children Learn*. London: Practical Pre-School Books.

Quinn, P.C. (2002) Early categorization: a new synthesis, in U. Goswami (ed.) (2002) *Blackwell Handbook of Childhood Cognitive Development*. Oxford: Blackwell Publishing.

Riedman, S.R. (1962) *The World Through Your Senses*, revised edn. London: Abelard-Schuman.

Roberts, A. and Featherstone, S. (2002) *The Little Book of Treasure Baskets*. Husbands Bosworth: Featherstone Education Ltd.

Schoen, S.A., Miller, L.J. and Green, K.E. (2008) Pilot study of the Sensory Over-Responsivity Scales: assessment and inventory, *American Journal of Occupational Therapy*, 62(4).

Shutts, K., Keen, R., Ornkloo, H., von Hofsten, C. and Spelke, E.S. (2009) Young children's representations of spatial and functional relations between objects, *Child Development*, 80(6): 1612–27.

Sigman, A. (2011) Close encounters of the green kind, *Montessori International*, April–June: 40.

Sims, C.E. (2006) Uses of information in categorization: does task matter? Unpublished thesis, University of California Davis.

Siraj-Blatchford, I. and Sylva, K. (2004) Researching pedagogy in English pre-schools, *British Educational Research Journal*, 30(5).

Smith, A. (1984) *The Mind*. Harmondsworth: Penguin Books.

Smith Roley, S., Imperatore, B. and Schaaf, R.C. (eds) (2001) *Understanding the Nature of Sensory Integration with Diverse Populations*. San Antonio, TX: Therapy Skill Builders.

Sparrow, M. (2011) What can I do for my CVI child? *One Problem, Ten Solutions: A Handbook for Parents and Teachers*. Unpublished paper.

Stroh, K., Robinson, T. and Proctor, A. (2008) *Every Child Can Learn*. London: Sage Publications.

Sylva, K., Melhuish, M., Sammons, P. and Siraj-Blatchford, I. (2004) *The Effective Provision of Pre-school Education (EPPE) Project: Final Report*. London: Institute of Education.

Tickell, C. (2011) *The Early Years: Foundations for Life, Health and Learning – An Independent Report on the Early Years Foundation Stage to Her Majesty's Government*. London: Department of Education.

Usher, W. (2010) *Sensory Play Resource Book*. London: KIDS.

Vygotsky, L.S. (1978) *Mind in Society: The Development of Higher Psychological Processes*. London: Harvard University Press.

White, J. (ed.) (2011) *Outdoor Provision in the Early Years*. London: Sage Publications.

Whitebread, D. and Bingham, S. (2011) *School readiness: a critical review of perspectives and evidence*, TACTYC Occasional Paper No. 2. np: TACTYC.

Wilbarger, P. and Wilbarger, J. (1991) *Sensory Defensiveness in Children Aged 2–12: An Intervention Guide for Parents and Other Caregivers*. Denver, CO: Avanti Educational Programmes.

Wilkening, F. and Huber, S. (2002) Children's intuitive physics, in U. Goswami (ed.) *Blackwell Handbook of Childhood Cognitive Development*. Oxford: Blackwell Publishing.

Wing, L. (1992) *The Triad of Impairments of Social Interaction: An Aid to Diagnosis*. London: NAS.

Wood, E. (2010) Developing integrated pedagogical approaches to play and learning, in P. Broadhead, J. Howard and E. Wood (eds) *Play and Learning in the Early Years*. London: Sage Publications.

Index

Page numbers shown in *italics* refer to figures and tables.

acquisition, rule
  role of SPC in enabling, 106–7
actions *see* behaviours
activities, structured
  use for improving SEN access to treasure
    baskets, *136*
Activity Methods for Children under Eight
  (Anderson), 108
adult-initiated play
  features and role as stage in sensory play
    continuum, 85–8, *87*
adults
  and environment and child relations in
    quality play, 140–41, *140*
  balancing involvement of in child play,
    3, 163
  exploring sensory preferences of, 3–4
  importance of respect and behaviours of,
    152
  role in sensory play continuum 156, *157*
  role in sensory processing diagnosis,
    136–8
  salience of assumptions and expectations
    of, 144–5
  salience of presence for sensory play,
    146–8
  salience of reassurance and support of,
    148–50
agency and control
  salience in sensory play, 153–5
analysis, object
  salience in baby development, 43–4
Anderson, L., 17, 123
Anderson, M., 77, 108
appraisal
  importance in quality sensory play,
    140–41, *140*
arts and design, expressive
  salience as element of EYFS, 117–18
ASD (autism spectrum disorders)
  coping strategies for challenging actions,
    131–2

sensory problems and, 130–31
assumptions and expectations, adult
  salience in relation to sensory play,
    144–5
attention restoration theory
  as mode of appreciating qualities of
    nature, 8
auditory senses
  importance and role in processing
    information, 31–3
  making of as element of treasure basket
    object play, 67
  maximizing appeal of treasure basket
    objects to, *57*
autism spectrum disorders (ASD)
  coping strategies for challenging actions,
    131–2
  sensory problems and, 130–31
awareness, self-
  salience as outcome of PSED, 109–11

babies and toddlers
  case studies of SPC experiences, 89–103
  hearing characteristics and parameters,
    32–3
  role of categorisation in learning of,
    46–7
  salience of imitation and interpretation
    behaviours, 44–5
  salience of object recognition, analysis
    and permanence, 43–4
  salience of reasoning and analytical
    thinking, 45–6
  salience of sense of touch in information
    processing, 23–6, *24*, *25*
  taste characteristics and parameters, 31
  vision characteristics and parameters,
    29–30
  see also children
  see also features of e.g. brains
Baillargeon, R., 4, 6, 47, 48
Barton, G., 23

baskets, treasure
  balancing child- and adult-led play
    involving, 3, 163
  benefits to older children of play
    involving,162
  contribution of neuroscience to
    understanding of, 43
  definition and benefits, 52–3
  design criteria and role, 37–9, 53–4
  history and characteristics, 1–4, 5
  implications of learning tools for, 43
  importance and uses in SEN learning,
    133–6, 135–6
  role in priming children for exploration,
    8–9
  template of observation form for,
    164–5
  see also objects, treasure basket
  see also purposes e.g. heuristic play;
    sensory play
  see also tools enabling better use e.g.
    sensory play continuum
  see also usefulness e.g. analysis, object;
    imitation, behaviour; interpretation,
    behaviour; reasoning; recognition,
    object; thinking, analytical
Beaver, M., 113
behaviours
  characteristics of treasure basket object,
    63–9, 65
  importance of appropriate adult for
    sensory play, 152
  management of as target of PSED,
    111–12
  salience of baby imitation and
    interpretation of, 44–5
  see also schema, behaviour
  see also particular e.g. imitation,
    behaviour; learning; reasoning;
    thinking, analytical
Biel, M., 131, 152
Bogdashina, O., 1, 35, 35
Bornstein, M., 50–51
brains
  characteristics, 18
  role of baby brains in sensory play
    enhancement, 2, 161
  salience in sensory development, 9–10, 9
  see also outcomes using e.g. analysis,
    object; interpretation, behaviour;
    reasoning; thinking, analytical

see also tasks e.g. processing, sensory
  information; reception, sensory
  information; transmission, sensory
  information
Brierley, J., 9, 18
Broadhead, P., 41
Brown, F., 81
Bruner, J., 49
Butterworth, G., 19–20, 23

capabilities, child
  salience of observing to ensure sensory
    play, 152
case studies
  role and importance of EYFS curriculum,
    118–20
  sensory play continuum experiences,
    89–103
categorisation
  characteristics and usefulness of
    informational, 48–9
  role in learning of babies, 46–7
  role of SPC in enabling process, 106–7
Cat in the Hat, The (Seuss), 32
centres, activity
  relevance as location for behaviour
    schema, 50
children
  balancing child- and adult-led play, 3,
    163
  benefits to older children of treasure
    basket play,162
  case studies of SPC experiences, 89–103
  characteristics of older child approach to
    SPC, 105–6, 105
  extent and nature of SPC involvement,
    103–4
  relationship with adults and
    environment in quality play, 140–41,
    140
  responses to sensory play, 10–13
  salience of observing capabilities and
    needs of, 152
  see also babies and toddlers
CL (communication and language)
  characteristics as prime area of EYFS,
    112–14
collections, themed
  comparison with treasure basket objects,
    71–3
  role in sensory play, 70–71

communication
  salience as element of treasure basket
    object play, 68
  see also specific e.g. sounds, making of
communication and language (CL)
  characteristics as prime area of EYFS,
    112–14
communities and people
  salience as element of UW, 116–17
compartmentalization
  characteristics and usefulness of
    informational, 48–9
  role in learning of babies, 46–7
  role of SPC in enabling process, 106–7
concerns
  usefulness of play objects as representing
    and expressing, 40–41
confidence, self-
  salience as outcome of PSED, 109–11
contents, treasure basket *see* objects,
    treasure basket
contexts
  case studies of role and importance in
    EYFS learning, 118, 120
  of SPC case studies, 89, 90, 91, 92, 93–4,
    96, 97, 99, 100
Coronation Street, 32
cortex, visual
  importance and role in processing
    information, 28–9
continuums, sensory play *see* sensory play
    continuums
control and agency
  salience in sensory play, 153–5
Crowe, B., 12–13, 20, 31, 33
Cubey, P., 50
cues, emotional
  salience in relation to sensory play,
    148
curricula
  role in moulding learning and teaching
    styles, 121–2
  role of sensory play in EYFS, 108–9
  three prime areas of EYFS, 109–14
  see also specific areas e.g. expressive arts
    and design; literacy; mathematics;
    understanding of the world
cycles, sensory play *see* sensory play
    continuums

De Casper, A., 32

depth
  criteria for ideal treasure basket, 53
design and arts, expressive
  salience as element of EYFS, 117–18
detail, focus on
  salience as feature of sensory processing
    disorder, 129–30
Developing Play for the under 3s (Hughes), 52
development, personal, social and
    emotional
  characteristics as prime area of EYFS,
    109–12
development, physical
  characteristics as prime area of EYFS, 114
diagnosis, sensory processing
  adult role in countering difficulties of,
    136–8
disorders, sensory
  and autism spectrum disorder, 130–31
  characteristics in SEN, 123–4
  see also problem areas e.g. processing,
    sensory information; reception,
    sensory information; transmission,
    sensory information

EAD (expressive arts and design)
  salience as element of EYFS, 117–18
Early Years Foundation Stage (EYFS)
  characteristics of sensory play within,
    108–9
  role in moulding learning and teaching
    styles, 121–2
  three prime areas of, 109–14
  see also specific areas e.g. expressive arts
    and design; literacy; mathematics;
    understanding of the world
Edgar, G., 36
education *see* learning
Emilia, R., 7
Emmons, P., 17, 123
emotions, development of
  characteristics as prime area of EYFS,
    109–12
encouragement, speech
  salience as target of CL, 113–14
engagement, child
  role of SPC in stimulating, 103–4, 105–6,
    105
environments
  and relationships to ensure quality
    sensory play, 140–41, *140*

features of to ensure quality sensory play, 141–2, 143–4
importance and uses of sensory in SEN learning, 132
importance of for successful treasure basket use, 60–61
see also resources
see also specific e.g. outdoors; rooms, sensory
Evans, G., 8
expectations and assumptions, adult salience in relation to sensory play, 144–5
experiential learning importance and object recognition and use in, 47–8
exploration and investigation
role of SPC in enhancing play and, 107
role of treasure baskets in priming children for, 8–9
salience as element of treasure basket object play, 65–6, 65
usefulness of play objects as representing and expressing, 41–2
see also imagination
expressive arts and design (EAD) salience as element of EYFS, 117–18
eyes importance and role in processing information, 27
EYFS *see* Early Years Foundation Stage

familiarisation usefulness of play objects as representing and expressing, 41–2
Fifer, W., 32
feedback, lack of salience as feature of sensory processing disorder, 127
feelings, human management of as target of PSED, 111–12
usefulness of play objects as representing and expressing, 40–41
flexibility salience as feature of sensory play, 14–15
Forbes, R., 19–20, 113, 146, 148
Forest schools movement, 7
free play strategies improving SEN access to treasure basket, 135

features and role as stage in sensory play continuum, 77–9
Froebel, F., 6

Garvey, C., 40
Gascoyne, S., 77–88, *80, 82, 83, 87*
gatekeepers, sensory lack of as feature of sensory processing disorder, 129
Geraghty, P., 7, 41–2, 143, 144, 153–4
Gibson, E., 36
Gibson, J., 4
Goldschmied, E., 1–2, 3, 5, 37, 52, 53, 54, 55, 56, 59, 73, 78, 79, 147
gustatory senses importance and role in processing information, 30–31
maximizing appeal of treasure basket objects to, *57*

habituation salience as feature of sensory processing disorder, 127
handles criteria for ideal treasure basket, 53
hands, human taxonomies of exploratory procedures, 25
Harris, M., 23
hearing importance and role in processing information, 31–3
heuristic play definition, features and theories supporting, 5
strengths and characteristics as sensory play type, 73–4
Hill, J., 133
Hughes, A., 32, 52, 59, 62
Hughes, F., 15, 155

imagination as element of EAD, 117–18
as element of treasure basket object play, 69
see also exploration and investigation
imitation, behaviour salience of baby engagement in, 44–5
infants *see* babies and toddlers
information characteristics and usefulness of categorization of, 48–9

information, sensory
  challenges posed in SEN, 124–6
  problems in ASD, 130–31
  see also processing, sensory information;
    reception, sensory information;
    transmission, sensory information
integration, lack of
  salience as feature of sensory processing
    disorder, 130
interaction, social
  usefulness of play objects as channel for,
    41
interests
  usefulness of play objects as representing
    and expressing, 40–41
interpretation, behaviour
  salience of baby engagement in, 44–5
interventions
  ensuring SEN access to treasure baskets,
    134, *135–6*
  importance of appropriate adult, 153,
    155–6
investigation *see* exploration and
    investigation
involvement, child
  role of SPC in stimulating, 103–4, 105–6,
    105
Involvement Scale for Young Children,
    103–4
Isaacs, S., 7

Jackson, S., 37

Kalliala, M., 139
kinaesthetic senses
  importance and role in processing
    information, 33–4
Klatzky, R., 24, 25, *25*, 66
Kurtz, A., 29, *30*

language and communication
  characteristics as prime area of EYFS,
    112–14
learning
  interventions ensuring SEN access to
    treasure basket, 134, 135–6
  messages provided by SPC case study
    behaviours, 90, 91, 92, 93, 95, 96–7, 98,
    99–100, 101–3
  role of categorization in baby, 46–7
  see also curricula

see also arenas e.g. outdoors; rooms,
    sensory
see also types e.g. experiential learning;
    imitation, behaviour
see also outcomes e.g. interpretation,
    behaviour; reasoning; thinking,
    analytical
Lederman, S., 24, 25, *25*, 66
Leuven Involvement Scale for Young
    Children, 41
Liben, L., 25
literacy
  salience as target of EYFS, 114–15
loose parts play
  definition, features and theories
    supporting, 5
  strengths and characteristics as sensory
    play type, 74–6

MacFarlane, A., 20
McInnes, K., 144, 147, 148, 156
MacMillan, M., 7
management
  salience of behaviour and feeling as
    target of PSED, 111–12
manipulation
  salience as element of treasure basket
    object play, 66–7
Mash, C., 50–51
matching, behaviour
  salience of baby engagement in, 44–5
materials
  criteria for ideal treasure basket, 53
  natural versus plastic for treasure basket
    objects, 59
  salience as element of EAD, 117–18
mathematics
  salience as target of EYFS, 115–16, *116*
Meade, A., 50
measurement
  salience as target of EYFS mathematics,
    115–16, *116*
media
  salience as element of EAD, 117–18
Meltzoff, A., 23, 45
messages, learning behaviour
  of SPC case studies, 90, 91, 92, 93, 95,
    96–7, 98, 99–100, 101–3
metal
  salience in relation to treasure basket
    objects, 72–3

Montessori, M., 6
movement
salience as element of treasure basket
object play, 64–5
see also specific e.g. exploration and
investigation; manipulation
Moyles, J., 115, 156
Murray, J., 42, 148

nature
attention theory as mode of appreciating
restorative qualities of, 8
importance and uses in SEN learning,
133
strengths and benefits as play
environment, 7–9
needs, child
salience of observing in sensory play, 152
needs, special educational *see* special
educational needs
nerves, optic
importance and role in processing
information, 27
neuroscience
contribution to understanding of objects
and treasure basket play, 43
see also brain, human
see also specific involvement e.g. analysis,
object; recognition, object
Nicholson, S., 5, 74–5
novelty
as key principle for treasure basket
objects, 59–60
numeracy
salience as target of EYFS mathematics,
115–16, *116*

objects
recognition, analysis and permanence of
in baby development, 43–4
objects, play
benefits and appeal of for play
enhancement, 2–3, 161–2
contribution of neuroscience to
understanding of, 43
design criteria and role, 39–40, 39
history and usefulness, 14
use in symbolic play, 42–3
see also objects, treasure basket
see also representation and usefulness e.g.
concerns; exploration and

investigation; familiarisation; feelings,
human; interaction, social; interests;
learning; understanding
objects, themed
comparison with treasure basket objects,
71–3
role in sensory play, 70–71
role of collections of in sensory play,
70–71
objects, treasure basket
benefits and appeal of objects of, 56–8,
56, 57, 161–2
comparison with themed objects, 71–3
design criteria and role of, 39–40, *39*
ideal quantity and quality of, 54–6
key principles of successful, 59–60
salience of environments for successful
use, 60–61
selection of as element in sensory play
continuum, 81, *82, 83*
stages of play with, 62–3
suitable recipients of play with, 69–70
typical play behaviours with, 63–9, *65*
observation and reflection
case studies of role and importance in
EYFS learning, 119, 120
form template for treasure basket, *164–5*
importance for sensory play, 158–9
of SPC case studies, 90–91, 91–2, 92–3,
94–5, 96, 97–8, 99, 100–101
olfactory sense
importance and role in processing
information, 19–22
maximizing appeal of treasure basket
objects to, *57*
open-endedness
salience as feature of sensory play, 13–14
outdoors
attention theory as mode of appreciating
restorative qualities of, 8
importance and uses in SEN learning,
133
strengths and benefits as play
environment, 7–9

Papatheodorou, T., 65, 89, 104, 110–11
PD (physical development)
characteristics as prime area of EYFS, 114
People under Three (Goldschmied), 37
perception, sensory
stages and characteristics, 35–6

people and communities
  salience as element of UW, 116–17
permanence, object
  salience in baby development, 44
personal, social and emotional
    development (PSED)
  characteristics as prime area of EYFS,
    109–12
Peske, N., 131, 152
Pestalozzi, J., 6
physical development (PD)
  characteristics as prime area of EYFS,
    114
Piaget, J., 5–6, 44, 62
Pike, G., 36
planning
  importance for sensory play, 158–9
plastic
  vs. natural materials for treasure basket
    objects, 59
play
  characteristics of treasure basket object,
    63–9, *65*
  historical comparison of children's,
    10–13
  stages of treasure basket object, 62–3
  suitable recipients of treasure basket
    object, 69–70
  see also type e.g. adult-initiated play; free
    play; heuristic play; loose parts play;
    'pretend' play; sensory play; symbolic
    play
Play Culture in a Changing World (Kalliala),
    139
Play England, 147
presence, adult
  salience in relation to sensory play,
    146–8
'pretend' play
  as element of treasure basket object play,
    69
  SPC and, 104–5
problems, solving of
  salience as element of treasure basket
    object play, 68–9
processing, sensory information
  and autism spectrum disorder, 130–31
  and perception, 34–5, *35*
  challenges of as element of SEN, 126
  definition and characteristics, 19–34, *24*,
    25, 123–4

see also diagnosis, sensory processing;
    reception, sensory information;
    transmission, sensory information
see also key manifestations e.g. detail, focus
    on; feedback, lack of; gatekeepers,
    sensory; habituation; integration, lack
    of; stimulation, over- and under-
proprioception senses
  importance and role in processing
    information, 33–4
PSED (personal, social and emotional
    development)
  characteristics as prime area of EYFS,
    109–12

quality
  ideal for treasure basket objects, 55–6
quantity
  ideal for treasure basket objects, 54–5
questions and questioning
  salience as treasure basket object play
    stage, 62–3

reading
  salience as target of EYFS literacy,
    114–15
reasoning
  baby engagement in qualitative and
    quantitative, 46
reassurance and support, adult
  salience in relation to sensory play,
    148–50
reception, sensory information
  challenges of as element of SEN, 124–6
  see also processing, sensory information;
    transmission, sensory information
recognition, object
  salience in baby development, 43–4
  use within experiential learning, 47–8
reflection *see* observation and reflection
reflexes
  role in reception of sensory information,
    125–6
relationships
  between environment, child and adult in
    quality play, 140–41, *140*
  salience of personal as target of PSED,
    112
relevance
  salience as feature of sensory play,
    15–16

resources
  salience of attractive and stimulating in
    quality play, 142–3
  salience of combining as stage in sensory
    play continuum, 80–85, *80, 82, 83*
  see also environments
  see also specific e.g. baskets, treasure
respect, by adults
  importance in sensory play, 152
risk and safety
  salience in relation to sensory play,
    150–51
rooms, sensory
  importance and uses in SEN learning,
    132
Roopnarine, J., 15
rules, acquisition of
  role of SPC in enabling, 106–7

safety and risk
  salience in relation to sensory play,
    150–51
scale, environment
  importance in quality play, 143–4
schema, behaviour
  importance and characteristics, 49–51
selection
  importance of play selection in adult-
    initiated play, 85–6
  treasure basket object as element of
    sensory play continuum, 81, *82, 83*
SEN *see* special educational needs
senses, human
  brain in development of, 9–10, *9*
  characteristics and uses, 18–19, *19*
  exploring adult preferences of, 3–4
  importance as driver enhancing play, 2,
    163
  treasure basket objects to appeal to, 56–8,
    56, 57
  see also information, sensory; perception,
    sensory; sensory play; stimulation,
    sensory
  see also particular and type e.g. hearing;
    kinaesthetic senses; proprioception
    senses; sight; smell; taste; touch;
    vestibular senses
sensory play
  balancing child- and adult-led, 3, 163
  benefits, features and importance, 13–15,
    162

children's responses to, 10–13
connections between treasure baskets
  and, 4
considerations for supporting child
  capabilities and needs, 151–6
importance as driver enhancing play, 2,
  161
role in EYFS, 108–9
role of SPC in enhancing exploration
  and, 107
theoretical underpinnings for promotion
  of, 5–7
see also objects, play; objects, treasure
  basket
see also arenas e.g. outdoors
see also elements e.g. collections, themed
see also factors ensuring successful e.g.
  appraisal; environments; observation
  and reflection; planning; presence,
  adult; reassurance and support;
  relationships; resources; time
see also factors influencing negatively e.g.
  assumptions and expectations, adult;
  safety and risk
Sensory Play (Papatheodorou), 89
sensory play continuums (SPCs)
  as mechanism for engaging older
    children, 70
  benefits and features, 15–16, *16*
  case studies of child experience of,
    89–103
  extent and nature of children's
    involvement, 103–4, 105–6, *105*
  need for flexibility of stages, 156–8
  'pretend' play and, 104–5
  role in enabling rule acquisition,
    106–7
  role in enhancing play and exploration,
    107
  role of adults, 156, *157*
  stages and characteristics, 77–88, *80, 82,*
    83, 87
  use for SEN access to treasure baskets,
    134, *135–6*
Sensory Play Research Project, xi
Seuss, Dr., 32
shape
  criteria for ideal treasure basket, 53
  salience as target of EYFS mathematics,
    115–16, *116*
Shutts, K., 115

sight
  importance and role in processing
    information, 26–30
  maximising appeal of treasure basket
    objects to, *57*
simplicity
  salience as feature of sensory play, 13
size
  criteria for ideal treasure basket, 53
skills, personal, social and emotional
  development of as prime area of EYFS,
    109–12
smell
  importance and role in processing
    information, 19–22
  maximizing appeal of treasure basket
    objects to, *57*
Smith, A., 18
Social Play Continuum (Broadhead), 41
social skills
  development of as prime area of EYFS,
    109–12
sounds
  importance and role in processing
    information, 31–3
  making of as element of treasure basket
    object play, 67
  maximizing appeal of treasure basket
    objects to, *57*
space
  importance of environmental in quality
    play, 143–4
  salience as target of EYFS mathematics,
    115–16, *116*
Sparrow, M., 130
SPCs *see* Sensory Play Continuums
special educational needs (SEN)
  coping strategies for challenging actions,
    131–2
  features of sensory information
    disorders, 123–4
  importance and uses of outdoors
    learning, 133
  need for appropriate sensory stimulation,
    132–4
  salience and uses of treasure baskets,
    133–6, *135–6*
  sensory information challenges facing,
    124–6
  see also problem areas e.g. processing,
    sensory information; reception,

sensory information; transmission,
    sensory information
  see also specific disorders e.g. autism
    spectrum disorders
speech
  understanding and encouraging as target
    of CL, 113–15
Steiner, R., 6
stimulation, over- and under-
  salience as feature of sensory processing
    disorder, 127–9
stimulation, sensory
  need for appropriate in SEN, 132–4
  see also tools e.g. baskets, treasure
structure, activity
  use for improving SEN access to treasure
    baskets, *136*
support and reassurance, adult
  salience in relation to sensory play,
    148–50
Sylva, K., 149–50, 156
symbolic play
  use of play objects in, 42–3

tactile senses
  importance and role in processing
    information, 22–6, *24*, *25*
  maximizing appeal of treasure basket
    objects to, *57*
taste
  importance and role in processing
    information, 30–31
  maximizing appeal of treasure basket
    objects to, *57*
taxonomies
  exploratory hand procedures, 25
templates
  form for treasure basket observation,
    164–5
theories
  attention restoration theory and
    restorative nature, 8
  underpinning promotion of sensory play,
    5–7
thinking, analytical
  salience of baby engagement in, 45
Tickell, C., 113
time
  salience of sufficient in sensory play,
    146
toddlers *see* babies and toddlers

tools, learning
  definition and implications for treasure
    basket play, 43
  role of objects in notion of, 40
touch
  importance and role in processing
    information, 22–6, *24, 25*
  maximizing appeal of treasure basket
    objects to, *57*
toys
  vs. non-toys for treasure basket objects,
    59
transmission, sensory information
  challenges of as element of SEN, 126
  see also processing, sensory information;
    reception, sensory information
treasure, baskets of *see* baskets, treasure

understanding
  salience of speech as target of CL,
    113–14
  usefulness of play objects as representing
    and expressing, 41–2
Understanding Sensory Dysfunction
  (Emmons), 17, 123

understanding the world (UW)
  salience as element of EYFS, 116–17
Usher, W., 4

vestibular senses
  importance and role in processing
    information, 33–4
visual senses
  importance and role in processing
    information, 26–30
  maximizing appeal of treasure basket
    objects to, *57*

Waldon, G., 40, 43
weave
  criteria of for ideal treasure basket, 53
Wells, N., 8
White, J., 117, 142, 146
Williams, D., 129
Wood, E., 148
Worthington, M., 156
writing
  salience as target of EYFS literacy, 114–15
world, understanding of
  salience as element of EYFS, 116–17

**THE ROLE OF THE ADULT
IN EARLY YEARS SETTINGS**

Janet Rose and Sue Rogers

9780335242306 (Paperback)
July 2012

eBook also available

This essential book focuses on the adult role within early years
education and care. The book introduces the concept of the 'plural
practitioner', which acknowledges that the role of the adult in early
years settings is complex and entails many different responsibilities.

Key features:

- Discussion of the seven different dimensions of the adult role - to
  help practitioners reflect on the multiple and complex ways in
  which they work with young children
- Key questions at the end of each chapter to stimulate further
  reflection and reading
- Case study examples of real practitioner experiences

www.openup.co.uk

OPEN UNIVERSITY PRESS
McGraw - Hill Education

DOING ETHICAL RESEARCH WITH CHILDREN

Deborah Harcourt and
Jonathon Sargeant
9780335246427 (Paperback)

August 2012

eBook also available

Doing Ethical Research with Children introduces students to the key considerations involved when researching with children and young people, from both a methodological and ethical perspective. It will assist students as they develop, conduct and disseminate research that relates to children and childhood.

Key features:

- Combines appropriate and supportive information to offer a guide through the issues and essential elements of conducting ethical research with children
- Includes pedagogical features throughout to develop understanding
- Different stages of research are covered, from planning the research to carrying out the study

www.openup.co.uk

 OPEN UNIVERSITY PRESS
McGraw - Hill Education

OBSERVATION
Origins and Approaches
in Early Childhood

Valerie Podmore and Paulette Luff

9780335244249 (Paperback)
2012

eBook also available

"This book is an excellent resource for all those studying or working in the field of early childhood. It deals with key issues of observational processes offering a balance between theory and practical activities. It is written in a critical, engaging and informative way, with scope for interesting discussions with students, and is a useful tool for lecturers and students as in learning about observations for all involved in early childhood education."
Dr. Ioanna Palaiologou, Lecturer, University of Hull, UK

Key features:

- An adaptation of a book that has been successful in New Zealand – updated with UK content
- Rich in examples, drawing on a variety of studies, policies and contexts to illustrate key points
- A range of practical techniques, both qualitative and quantitative for practitioners

www.openup.co.uk

OPEN UNIVERSITY PRESS
McGraw - Hill Education